From

The Women
124 Shoreditch Higl

CW00661215

Sarah Hopkins. 'I have been involved in Greenham's support network since the beginning and was drawn to work on this book because what is happening at Greenham is too important to go unrecorded.

'I live in Dorset. What I enjoy most are the people in my life, writing and politics. I am an idealist and an optimist, and proud of both. They have served me well.

'Greenham women have been presented by the media as either angels or devils. I hope this book puts you in touch with us.'

Barbara Harford is a freelance journalist and writer. Since she became involved with the Women's Peace Camp in 1982 she has become actively committed to women's issues within the context of broader-based struggles. As a feminist it is her conviction that women's issues are fundamental to the struggle for a sane and balanced society. 'I think it is crucial that women speak as loudly and as often as we can. We must create our own actions and write our own herstory to shape the identities and the world that we ourselves desire.'

BARBARA HARFORD
SARAH HOPKINS

# Greenham Common:
# Women at the Wire

 The Women's Press

*This book is dedicated to all our oppressors. Your time is up!*

First published by The Women's Press Limited 1984
A member of the Namara Group
124 Shoreditch High Street, London E1 6JE

British Library Cataloguing in Publication Data

Greenham Common: Women at the Wire
1. Peace–Societies, etc.
2. Women and peace
3. Greenham Common (Berkshire) – History
I. Harford, Barbara    II. Hopkins, Sarah
327.1'72'088042    JX1965

ISBN 0–7043–3926–9

Typeset by M.C. Typeset, Chatham, Kent
Printed in Great Britain by Nene Litho
and bound by Woolnough Bookbinding
both of Wellingborough, Northants.

# Contents

# Acknowledgements

Putting this book together has not been easy. It has been an action to which many women have given much.

We received enough writing for three volumes. So after the joy and exhilaration of reading it, came the agony of creating a book. Restrictions of space meant we had to extract many women's work, which was painful for us all.

We have over 50 women's writing here, but it still leaves lots of our experiences and feelings untold. This book is only a beginning. Women at Greenham and elsewhere will continue putting our voices into the world, with the kind of courage and determination that makes things change.

We would like to thank everyone who has helped us in our part of the job by typing, advising, transcribing, doing mapwork and research, taping, consoling, photographing and letting us take over their homes so that we could work: Jayne, Eleanor, Sarah B., Kim, Lisa, Charlie, Sue, Judy, Marijke, Theresa, Rowan, Mary, Ioma, Frannie, Chris and Colin. Thank you to all the wonderful women who have contributed their time and energy in sharing their experiences with us. Particular thanks to Aggie and Babs who helped with editorial work.

Acknowledgements also to Gill Hanscombe whose help has been both exhilarating and essential in transforming a pile of papers into a book! We'd like to thank our publisher, Ros de Lanerolle, too, for her trust, encouragement and patience throughout the year.

*Barbara Harford*
*Sarah Hopkins*

# Dateline

1981

*27 Aug* 'Women for Life on Earth' march leaves Cardiff.

*5 Sept* March arrives at Greenham.

*21 Dec* First action: women stop sewage pipes being laid.

1982

*18 Jan* Women keen outside House of Commons on re-opening of Parliament.

*20 Jan* Newbury District Council serves notice of intention to evict camp from common land.

*Early Feb* Camp becomes women only.

*21 Mar* Equinox Festival of Life.

*22 Mar* First blockade of base by 250 women. 34 arrests.

*Mar–May* Spot blockades.

*27 May* First eviction from common land. Camp re-sited on MOT land. 4 women arrested.

*28 May* Eviction trial. 4 women imprisoned.

*7 June* 75 women die symbolically outside London Stock Exchange to point up profits made from arms race as President Reagan visits Britain. 7 women arrested.

*6 Aug* Hiroshima Day. Women place 10,000 stones on Newbury War Memorial.

*9 Aug* Nagasaki Day. 8 women enter base to present Commander with the 1000th origami crane, a symbol of peace.

*27 Aug* 18 women occupy the main gate sentry box until arrested.

*29 Sept* Eviction from Ministry of Transport land.

*5 Oct* Obstruction of work to lay sewage pipes. 13 arrested.

*15 Nov* Sentry box action trial.
*17 Nov* Sewage pipe action trial.    23 women imprisoned.

*12 Dec* 30,000 women link hands to encircle the base.

*13 Dec* 2,000 women blockade the base. Some enter to plant snowdrops.

1983

*1 Jan* 44 women climb the fence to dance on the Cruise missile silos.

*17 Jan* At reopening of Parliament 73 women occupy the lobby of the Houses of Parliament to emphasise demands that the issue of Cruise missiles be debated.

*20 Jan* Second camp set up at Green Gate.

*22 Jan* First attempt to set up the Blue Gate camp. 3 arrests.

*7 Feb* Over 100 women enter base as snakes. Secretary of State for Defence, Heseltine, visits Newbury. Action at Council chambers.

*15 Feb* Silo action trials. 36 women imprisoned.

*22 Feb* High Court injunctions and eviction hearing adjourned when 400 women present affidavits stating that Greenham is their home.

*25 Feb* 6 women climb on to roof of Holloway women's prison to draw attention to the racial, class and economic injustices for which the imprisoned women are victimised.

*8 Mar* International Women's Day.

*9 Mar* High Court injunctions and eviction hearing. Injunctions awarded against 21 women.

*24 Mar* Visit of NATO Generals to base – women blockade.

*28 Mar* Holloway action trial. Women give evidence of inhumane treatment in prison. Charges against the 6 women dismissed.

*31 Mar* CND blockade the base.

*1 Apr* 200 women enter the base disguised as furry animals to have a picnic. CND link-up – 70,000 form a human chain linking Aldermaston, Burghfield and Greenham.

*27 Apr* Citadel locks action. All gates padlocked by women.

*1 May* Children's party on the common and inside the base.

*12 May* Eviction from common land at Yellow (main) Gate. Women's cars illegally impounded.

*24 May* International Women's Day for Disarmament. Silent vigil and fasting at Greenham.

*31 May* Women dressed in black enter base to scatter ashes as US Cruise technicians arrive.

*25 June* Rainbow Dragon Festival. 2000 women sew 4½-mile serpent tail that weaves in and out of the base.

*4–9 July* Week of blockades. Women enter to make personal rituals. Christian exorcism performed. Culminates in removal of 50 ft of fence. New camps set up at Orange and Blue Gates.

*24 July* Women die symbolically in front of the public, politicians and military buyers who have come to view war hardware on display at an Air Tattoo at Greenham.

*25 July* 7 women cut hole in fence and paint women's peace symbols on US spy plane 'Blackbird'.

*6 Aug* Hiroshima Day. Arrival of 20 'Stop The Arms Race' marches from all over UK. Silent vigil and fasting at Newbury War Memorial.

*9 Aug* Nagasaki Day. Die-in at Yellow Gate. Women's outlines painted on road.

*18 Aug* 'Blackbird' trial. Charges withdrawn by MOD. One woman imprisoned for contempt.

*5 Sept* Second birthday celebrations. Women obstruct laying of fuel pipes into base. 27 arrests.

*6 Sept* Sabotage of fuel pipe workers' machinery.

*29 Oct* Halloween. 2,000 women take down 4 miles of fence. 187 arrests with increased violence from police and army.

*1 Nov* Heseltine tells House of Commons that 'intruders' near missile silos run risk of being shot at.

*9 Nov* Start of Federal court action in New York against President Reagan and George Bush to ban them from employing Cruise missiles in Britain. 24-hour vigils begin at all 102 US bases in Britain.

*13 Nov* Demonstration to honour the memory of Karen Silkwood, 9 years dead.

*14 Nov* First of the missile-carrying transporters arrive at Greenham. Night watches begin to check on Cruise activity. 18 peace activists in Turkey sentenced for 5–8 years' imprisonment.

*15 Nov* Blockade of all gates leads to 143 arrests.

*11 Dec* 50,000 women encircle the base, reflecting it back on itself with mirrors. Parts of the fence pulled down. Hundreds of arrests as police violence escalates – beatings, broken bones, concussions.

*20 Dec* Camps at all gates but one. Violence from soldiers, all-night harassment to prevent sleep, horrendous language amounting to verbal rape. Bricks and stones thrown at benders.

*27 Dec* 3 women spend 3 hours undetected in air traffic control tower.

*31 Dec* Final gate (Indigo) camped. New Year's party.

1984
*1 Jan* Women weave giant web, symbol of strength and fragility, to
float over base lifted by helium-filled balloons.
*5 Mar* MOT, NDC and MOD combine forces to commence programme of evictions, starting at north side of base in preparation for
Cruise convoy deployment.
*9 Mar* 12.30 a.m. 100 policemen with dogs converge on 12 women
at Blue Gate to prevent them alerting other camps that part of a
Cruise convoy (only 3 vehicles) has left the base. Despite police
efforts women manage to clock the convoy's route an hour later.

# Introduction

The Women's Peace Camp at Greenham Common wasn't planned. The events and people that made it happen were brought together by the 1981 'Women for Life on Earth' march from Cardiff to the United States Air Force (USAF) base at Greenham. Frustration at the media's disinterest, the determination of the marchers and the enthusiasm and help of supporters combined to create a continuing outdoor settlement that has survived three winters, numerous evictions and violent attacks from hostile groups.

What brought people to Greenham Common? Why have so many women been drawn to the camp? What is it like to live there? What has it taught us about ourselves?

The marchers and the people who first came to join the camp were motivated and united by the horror of American Cruise missiles coming to Britain in accordance with a NATO decision taken on 12 December 1979. At Greenham, nuclear weapons are no longer abstract, hidden in statistics, tested in faraway places. If you are at the wire around the base you can actually see the relentless preparations for nuclear war going on each and every day on the other side of a fence guarded by British soldiers fronting for the invaders.

It is not that the coming of Cruise represents the only or greatest threat to the extent and quality of our lives, but that a group of people organised themselves around that particular issue making it a national focus. Their active response brought disarmament to life . . . you can actually see the evil you are up against when you are at Greenham, while so many other things that diminish and damage us are invisible. Over the months, Cruise has become a symbol of nuclear terror, male domination and imperialist exploitation. Our oppression is no longer abstract and that's why the protest at Greenham has led so many people into new realms of analysis and action.

1

Many early arrivals at the camp had political commitments, while others were disillusioned with conventional party politics as a democratic and effective way to run a country according to the needs and conscience of its people. The Women's Peace Camp became a place where ideas, fears, dreams, philosophies and skills came together to be worked through, causing disruption as well as exhilaration. It kept growing because so many people identify with the desperation that drives others to give up their normal comforts to challenge the way things are. It was a new development in the peace movement and one that continues to be controversial in terms of disarmament and feminism. Yet it has become central to both.

It began as a predominantly white, middle-class movement, but as it grew, the barriers of race, class and sexuality began to break down. More working-class women and lesbian women became involved and by the autumn of 1983 we were beginning to have dialogue with women of colour. The labels that divide women are being challenged together with the institutions that promote these divisions. They are being exposed and rejected by women for the oppressive tactics they are.

Cruise missiles are only the tip of the iceberg. All that has led to their invention has to be tackled too if disarmament is to be possible and permanent. The connections between the nuclear arms race and the structure of our society need to be clarified. One of the women, Jayne Burton, describes these in terms of 'patriarchy'.

> Patriarchy literally means father rule – and once you spot it, it never goes away: the percentage of men who are involved in the military, the government, positions of power; and of course, there is God the Father, supposed creator of all life – the life force itself given the masculine gender. I think that it is very important – the language that we have, the labels we use, they permeate our thinking.

Within a male-dominated society, male-dominated institutions and stereotyped male values have determined how all our resources will be used. So we now have a military/industrial complex that cultivates racial fear to boost profits for a fast-expanding armaments trade.

We note with anger that while we make up one-half of the world's population and do two-thirds of its work, we get only one-tenth of its income and less than one-hundredth of its assets (UN Report

2

1980). Women's work is often unpaid and certainly underpaid. Our stolen wages subsidise the world military economy. Women, as a worldwide group, have no economic power and this is reflected in the wicked way our wealth is distributed. While Britain alone spent £11,200 million on armaments in 1982, 18 million children died of starvation. Britain's arms budget would have provided each of those children with £600.

From the very beginning of the camp the principle of working without hierarchies was established. Most of our experience in this divided world shows us that certain people are in charge and the rest are meant to follow. This is how nuclear weapons have been able to pile up virtually unhindered for 40 years. The same pattern often occurs in small groups trying to work together. We have grown up in a world where violence/domination is used to 'solve' problems both in the home and between groups of people called nations. We have learnt to compete with each other in school, sports, fashion, business, ideology, rather than to work co-operatively for the good of all.

So we are starting from scratch, developing attitudes and methods that make domination and opting out unnecessary. We try to give every woman a voice – as in meetings where every woman speaks in turn around the circle – and this makes us listen to each other. We are teaching each other in an intense way. And this means that women who have been identified by the press as spokeswomen have no more impact on decision-making than the women who may have arrived the day before. It is new to us, we fail often, but it must be done, for political change is deeper and more firm when there is personal change too.

Greenham has changed the lives of many women. Traditionally men have left home for the front-line of war. Now women are leaving home to work for peace. Peace isn't just about removing a few pieces of war furniture, or bringing about an international cease-fire; it is about the condition of our lives. Peace is the absence of greed and domination by a few over the rest of us. So the fight is bigger and longer than we thought! And women have a great deal to gain by it. Our whisperings now need to be shouted. For generations we have stored up our rage against men, whether they were our fathers, our bosses or our husbands . . . these are the relationships in which we all too often feel personally powerless. And for generations we have missed out on the love of other women . . . the chance to choose for ourselves, free of men's expectations

3

and demands, beyond the isolation of the nuclear family. That's why Greenham is a woman's place.

The women-only decision at Greenham was primarily a tactical one – and a gut reaction – by some, to what was happening at the camp at the time. The rationale followed as women began to experience the benefits of organising on our own. We don't need to justify our position since all people have the right to organise around their own needs and concerns. However, the discussion provoked by this issue can be useful, especially when it reveals the extent of the deep-rooted reactionary forces we are up against. We explore some of this antagonism in Chapter 3 and elsewhere in the book. The rightness and necessity of that decision has been borne out time and time again ever since. Thousands of women identify with Greenham because they see women taking initiative that builds on, rather than denies, women's strength. For many women it has been the first time in their lives that they have become politically involved.

When men look at the world, everywhere they see other men in positions of power, leadership, men being assertive – images that reinforce male self-esteem. Some men do this in ways which individuals might find morally unacceptable but there are many others who are seen doing things they respect and wish to emulate.

If you ask where in the world women can see other women doing something which they admire and respect and which gives them a sense of their own power and their own value, there are precious few places. We need to build a positive image of ourselves in a way that isn't so much anti-men as pro-women. And we need the space to do that.

The media have quite consistently and continuously avoided taking up our perspectives on war, racism and sexism. They have sought always to find one representative to simplify all our hopes and contrasting experience. So there has been a lot of confusion about what the camp stands for. The confusion has been inside the camp as well as outside because every woman stands for herself and we try to live in a way that is respectful of our differences. Which comes first, disarmament or feminism? It always had to be one or the other – prioritising. We say you can't have one without the other.

Various authorities have followed the media's example in searching for a simple way to undermine and destroy the changing consciousness that Greenham represents. They have even attemp-

4

ted to isolate a 'core' group by taking out injunctions against named women. They have found, to their cost, that you cannot simplify our diversity – it has only served to expand our numbers.

Living at Greenham seems like a challenge, an adventure. It makes few compromises with mainstream society, it is an alternative, an outdoor community of women. Living up against the fence means there is no switching off – the terror is on our doorstep. We experience autumn, winter, spring and summer as we've never experienced them before. Living outdoors is not impossible after all, though it has been hard at times. We gained gypsy knowledge and learnt to build warm, spacious, comfortable homes for ourselves – benders – that two women can build in an afternoon. We survived with the generous help of people sending and arriving with money, food and firewood. And we survived because we had to – what we are doing makes sense and what we have created at Greenham feels good and right. From our alternative reality, the world from which we come looks pale and comfortless. We have to transform it. Not by reforms, but by revolution. The tide is turning because women are making sure it does.

But the form of the revolution is crucial. We believe that the means must be consistent with the ends and this has promoted continuous discussion and self-examination about non-violence. Is it merely a tactic or does it have a more far-reaching analysis and application? Within this book we have pointed to some aspects of this debate, which is by no means resolved.

At Greenham a womanly culture is evolving. We have looked into women's lives long ago and far away and gained some insight into women's powers and their suppression. Our political awareness has been enriched by these influences. They are not distractions, they fill the gaps and connect us to other women's struggles in different times and places.

Beyond Greenham these connections are becoming tangible. This was demonstrated most vividly on 24 May 1983 and later on 9 November when 102 peace camps were set up in the UK. A loose network of women has grown within the UK and is extending beyond national boundaries to Europe, Australasia, America, Japan and Canada. It crosses artificially created ideological boundaries as well, into Eastern Europe.

There is no membership at Greenham and our newsletters are irregular. Communication is largely by word of mouth. But the growing recognition of our crisis is apparent in the proliferation of

5

women's peace camps which have been set up as far apart as Seneca Falls in New York State and Pine Gap in Central Australia.

Over the months the struggle has changed. The initial purpose of the camp was to protest against Cruise, but its role soon extended to include the preparation of women to bring about such changes. Now the emphasis has moved further towards preparing and politicising women and it would be more accurate to describe Greenham as a 'women's resistance camp'.

Over 50 contributors have written for this book, as well as many others who have not written but who have been interviewed and involved in discussions.

We have tried, by this means, to show the diversity of women involved, to give some inkling of the many different backgrounds and beliefs of the women at Greenham.

But there are many aspects of living within our community that we have been unable to cover in this book. Among these are the symbolism we have developed, and our spiritual enquiry, which would require a book in themselves.

So this is still not a definitive view. There is no way we can represent thousands of women, and as editors it is still our own interpretation which provides the themes. It is an attempt at capturing moments of women's experience during an open-ended story, with the voices of individual women woven together into the continual fabric that is Greenham.

# What is Greenham Common?

In 1938 Newbury Corporation purchased Greenham Common for the enjoyment of local people. Within a year, World War Two had begun and 900 acres of the Common became an airforce base for the Royal Air Force (RAF). In 1944 it was used for the launching of airborne troops into the invasion of Normandy.

Some years later the airfield fell into disuse but the Ministry of Defence (MOD) never returned it to the Council for use as a public amenity. By 1951 the land had been bought by the MOD against the wishes of the local authorities and residents. Then concrete and chain mesh went up to enclose an area to be used as a forward operational base for B47 nuclear bombers of the American Strategic Air Command.

By 1968 the base was formally leased by the Americans and was openly called USAF (United States Air Force) Greenham Common. Practically all the personnel there are still American but they now hide behind the British MOD and call themselves RAF Greenham Common, presumably to prevent us thinking seriously about American occupation.

Inside the perimeter fence, which has been strengthened, is a miniature American colony including a school, entertainment facilities and shopping centres. Greenham Common also serves as a distribution point for American forces' mail and supplies.

The construction of Cruise missile silos has been protected by three layers of fencing and watch towers. The base is now able to accommodate an extra 2–4,000 front-line troops. A report to the US Senate, and indeed, the contract given to Tarmac to construct the silos, reveals that the missile silos at Greenham are hardened to withstand shock waves from nuclear explosives of up to 200 lb per square inch to survive a one megaton explosion one-third of a mile away.

The work force used to carry out the construction work on the base has been almost totally non-unionised.

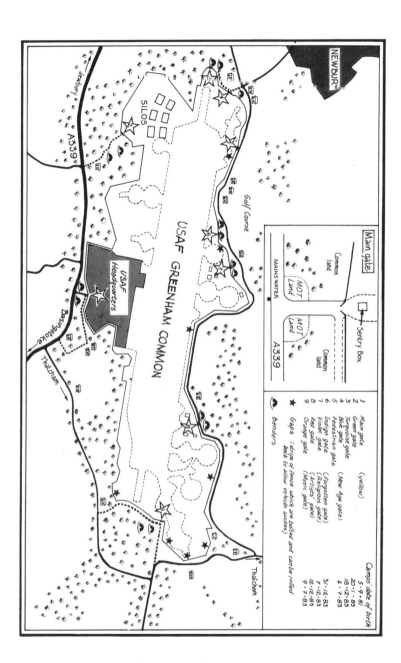

NEWBURY

A339

Newbury →

Basingstoke

Thatcham →

SILOS

USAF Headquarters

USAF GREENHAM COMMON

Golf Course

Common land

MAINS WATER

MOT Land

Common land

A339

Thatcham

**Main gate**

Sentry Box

| | | | |
|---|---|---|---|
| 1 | Main gate | (yellow) | |
| 2 | Green gate | | |
| 3 | Turquoise gate | | |
| 4 | Blue gate | (New Age gate) | |
| 5 | Pedestrian gate | | |
| 6 | Indigo gate | (Forgotten gate) | |
| 7 | Violet gate | (Religious gate) | |
| 8 | Red gate | (Artists' gate) | |
| 9 | Orange gate | (Music gate) | |

★ Gaps ('strips of fence which are bolted and can be rolled back to allow vehicle access')

▲ Benders

Camps' date of birth

5 · 9 · 81
20 · 1 · 83
18 · 12 · 83
4 · 7 · 83
31 · 12 · 83
7 · 12 · 83
12 · 12 · 83
9 · 7 · 83

# 1
# Awakening

1981. South Wales. It was here that the idea of a women-led march from Cardiff to Greenham, took shape and grew.

Women in Wales learned about a march organised and led by women that went from Scandinavia to Paris. The idea excited them. The anti-nuclear movement in Wales was growing and it was time for action.

'Why don't we do one like that?'

'We could make it mainly for women too . . .'

'Men could still support . . .'

'Yeah, they could help with the children and food on the way . . .'

'So that we'd be doing something in our own right, but not anti-men . . .'

'Just imagine . . . a load of ordinary unknown women marching from town to town, in protest against nuclear weapons . . .'

But no one wanted to take on the responsibility. The idea kept floating around in their minds until eventually, one by one, women committed themselves to it. A core group of four took on the main organisation for the march.

Where do you begin? The route. Two weeks would be long enough. A couple of women pored over a map and worked out a route.

'We ought to go to Greenham Common. That's where the first Cruise missiles are going to go after all . . .'

'And nobody knows where it is yet . . .'

'It's in Berkshire somewhere . . .'

'Well, we should make sure everyone knows exactly where it is because we are going to have to go there in our thousands.'

'Where is it?'

'Here.'

'Well, we can walk that far in two weeks, easily . . .'

'And visit other nuclear places on the way, to put them on the map, too.'

It began to feel as if it really would happen though there were only 12 weeks to organise the whole thing if it was going to be in the summer holidays. It was a slow start. Women had doubts about where to begin, how to begin, and how to overcome the feeling that they just hadn't enough time, or the right skills and strengths, or the stamina to keep it all going. It was a new and frightening responsibility to take on. Yet the actual organisation was quite straightforward common sense. It meant a lot of paperwork, sorting out publicity and telephoning around, but despite being hectic, it was manageable.

The Campaign for Nuclear Disarmament's (CND) response was disappointing at first. They were too busy to help. The idea of a women-led march didn't seem to interest them that much. Later on, they agreed to loan £250 to cover postage, posters and leaflets to distribute along the way.

Women's groups and peace groups in towns on the route were contacted. Most were ready with encouragement but hadn't the time to help with arrangements. Some women's groups wouldn't support because although the march was a women's initiative, it invited men to participate.

A meeting was held in Bristol – the halfway point – to bring together supporters from the various towns the march planned to pass through. But only three women were there and the woman whose house they were meeting in had already decided the march was too long and involved too much hard work.

But by then other things were coming together. The event had a name – 'Women for Life on Earth'. It was clear, bold, positive. A leaflet was designed. It was straight to the point. On one side was written, 'Why are we walking 120 miles from a nuclear weapons factory in Cardiff to a site for Cruise missiles in Berkshire?' On the back was a picture of a baby born dead and deformed – a victim of radiation from the Hiroshima explosion. It said, 'This is why'.

*Angela Phillips, a member of the Campaign Against Cruise Missiles in Newbury, the town nearest to Greenham Common, was one woman who turned up at the Bristol meeting:* I agreed to organise the final stages of the march because it was timed for the late summer and would be over before the new teaching term began. I remember feelings of resentment at 'losing' my precious

10

holiday and fear at what I had ~~taken~~ ~~on as the pressure of activity~~
increased. I had to make a series of car journeys to arrange food and accommodation; a simple enough task but I hadn't been driving long and I was nervous. There was publicity to organise, a bank account to be opened, a public address system to be hired, negotiations with the police over traffic arrangements . . . loads of tasks I'd never had to do before.

On 27 August 1981 36 women and four men, aged between 25 and 80, as well as a few children, set out to walk from Cardiff to Greenham. Four more joined on the way. For most of the marchers it was a radical move even to take ten days out of their normal lives and none of them envisaged what was to grow from those tentative beginnings. Most of them were not even clear about why they were going. It just felt like something they must do.

*The oldest walker was Effie Leah, who is in her seventies:* I'm not a very strong person for or against things, and I had never done anything before. I'd been on the alternative side of things – we grow tomatoes and shrubs for a market garden and where we live is rather remote. But I began to realise things had altered. The weapons were piling up and I began to feel I needed reassuring by being with other people. I heard about the march from a stallholder at a medieval fair. She gave me a phone number so I decided to ring up. I was feeling very nervous. I'd bought a suitcase, but while I was in Cardiff I changed it for a rucksack . . . I had decided to go.

*Helen John, a trained midwife and active in the Labour Party, decided to go too:* I've never approved of nuclear weapons or nuclear conflict, but I quite happily fell asleep while all the others who disliked them marched up and down the roads with banners. That was in the 60s. I could never understand what anyone hoped to achieve by marching from A to B and then going home. It didn't seem logical . . . so I was surprised to find I actually wanted to go on the march from Cardiff.

I changed because of the sudden realisation of what Cruise missiles coming to Europe actually meant. It first struck me at a meeting I went to . . . it was seeing all those young people there whose futures were going to be damaged, trying desperately to do something to stop it. My generation had really not worked hard enough to prevent this happening . . . It was a fit of guilt, I think,

11

that got me active.

The march appealed to me. I saw it as an opportunity to act very clearly as a woman and state that I didn't want to be defended by nuclear weapons. I wanted to show by joining in that I personally didn't accept what was going on.

*Liz Stoker is a social worker:* I saw an article in a women's glossy magazine. I'm 46 and my health hadn't been too good. I wanted to prove I could march that far. I didn't know a lot about the peace thing . . . I thought it would be a way of learning something . . . in fact there turned out to be a lot of people who were like me, so we did a lot of sharing.

*Ev Silver is an artist:* I'm 35 . . . I'd always been behind disarmament but never directly involved. It was when the Russians invaded Afghanistan, I suddenly thought . . . 'there's going to be a nuclear war'. Whenever those words had come up in my life before, I'd turned off, but this time I faced it and experienced the most horrible fears. My friends and I were making lots of lists and planning escape routes. Then I decided this was insane and there must be some other way I can handle this fear . . . I must get involved. I heard about the march on the grapevine . . . it seemed like the natural thing to do. The only way I can confront my fear and handle it is by being active. The march turned out to be a million times more inspiring than I'd thought. The luxury of having all that time to meet and talk things over with no time limits . . . I was confronting the two biggest fears in my life; that of nuclear war, and that of how far I dare go myself to stop it.

*The youngest walker was Jayne Burton who describes herself as a working-class woman:* When I first responded to the *Guardian* advert about the march my decision to go just sort of happened, but I know it was because it was a women-led march. What helped me to get it together, was being in a local CND group where there was a woman who didn't like working with men and made no secret of it. I was silently a bit shocked at her boldness but also very intrigued because I began to notice more how the group dynamics were or weren't working. I'd had no experience in the women's movement – apart from being a woman, of course – but for me the march was a follow-up to the intrigue that she awakened in me.

From Cardiff the marchers followed a route that took them through Newport, Caerwent (where there is a us army munitions dump) and Chepstow. Then they crossed the Severn Bridge to Bristol, Bath, Melksham, Devizes, Marlborough, and Hungerford. Before reaching Newbury they visited RAF Welford weapons store.

The marchers took their own sleeping bags and host groups in the different towns arranged accommodation and food in people's homes and village halls. A support vehicle accompanied the march with food and drink and room for extra baggage and tired children. For most of the time it was hot and dry and in some places a welcome swim had been arranged in the local swimming baths or a nearby river. Evenings were spent resting, making new friends, singing songs or having meetings. In some places their arrival was celebrated with a candlelit vigil.

The fact that the march was women-led and organised gave women the kind of pride and courage that helped them try new things.

*Jayne*: I remember on the march trying to overcome those internalised fears of speaking out for what I believed. Different women spoke at the places we stayed in. I remember speaking through a microphone at a shopping centre. Just a few people gathered round and other shoppers either scurried by totally disinterested or looked a bit baffled, bags in hand. It was the first time I'd spoken in public. It was a big step for me, but being with other women in an unaccustomed situation gave me the confidence to do it.

When we jubilantly walked into the Bath Peace Festival, singing and dancing, people stood up and applauded. It all felt very strange. Again some women from the march spoke and there was heckling when we broached the women's aspect of it. In fact there had been a hoo-ha about the women walking at the front, all along the way, but some women were really strong and determined that this should be so. I didn't really understand the fuss at the time – but I do now, and thank goodness for all the women who boldly speak out for their sisters. Special space and consideration for women doesn't just happen, it has to be worked for.

The marchers soon realised that their action was being completely ignored by the national press. Everyone felt it wasn't being taken seriously . . . something more needed to be done. But what?

A meeting was held to talk it through. Each person took a turn to say what they thought without comment from anyone else. Then everyone took their time to think over what had been said. It took three days and four long meetings to sort out.

*Angela*: Three days before the marchers were due to reach Greenham, three of them arrived at my house and began talking about chaining themselves to the perimeter fence of the base. They were excited and determined, I was scared. I hadn't had their experiences on the march, I'd been isolated from the solidarity and mutual support. We had an amazing meeting in Hungerford talking of arrests and prison sentences and body searches . . . about 15 of us crammed in a church hall kitchen. It wasn't exactly reassuring, but strength and commitment are infectious and I caught it. My last reservations disappeared when I joined the march late on the final afternoon.

It should have looked all ragged, a long straggling line of women and children tramping through the dusty Berkshire lanes with leaves in their hair. It should have seemed absurd, ineffectual. It didn't. There was too much energy and too much triumph about our successful arrival.

Nine days after they had left Cardiff the marchers reached Newbury on Friday, 4 September. Four women decided to do the chaining action, following the example set by the suffragettes. Another four women volunteered to be their helpers.

*Eunice Stellard, a proud grandmother, was among the first four to be chained up:* I hadn't slept much on Friday night. I imagined myself chained to the gate with guards with wire-cutters and dogs around me. I was positive I was going to be hurt. Then police cells and court and jail! I was glad to see the dawn break, to get going, get it done with and see it through. My grandson's sunhat and my granddaughter's sleeping bag and snapshots of my other grand-children made me feel they were near to me.

Greenham Common, when I first saw it, looked neat and tidy. The sun was shining. We parked the cars around the corner out of sight of the sentries. It was quiet and peaceful. When we got to the footpath we raced up to the gate. It was open so we chained ourselves to the fence at the side. Then Elspeth went back to

Newbury to tell the others we'd done it and to call the press.

*Jayne*: Minutes later a small group of women appeared dressed in black to 'keen'. They had a banner saying they were mourning for the children who may never have the chance to grow up. This was the first I'd heard of 'keening' but when they told me that it was wailing, lamenting – a way of expressing deep feelings of distress and anger – something in my being clicked and I joined in with them. It was like a healing, to wail out my distress and frustration at what the base represented.

An American woman, Merisa, kneeled next to me. As the sounds came deep from inside me there was a buzzing in my ears and I thought I was going to pass out – but instead the tears just flowed. Merisa was also crying and we put our arms around each other. For me it was like the completion of the whole experience of the march and chaining action. In fact, it was the completion of my whole life up to that point.

Meanwhile the rest of the marchers set out from Newbury to Greenham, but the police said they would not allow them to assemble at the main gate. There was nothing to be done but to keep on walking. No contingency plans had been made. Such last minute disappointments had not been expected, and little more was said about it.

At the last roundabout, women approached the police saying they had planned to get to the main gate and would the police take them there? They said yes! The 'March Magic' had worked again.

They had just two miles to go along the busy tree-lined A339 before reaching the left-hand turning to the base. When they got to the corner, their destination was clearly visible, only 20 yards away up a wide road edged with short-cropped privet hedges. Either side of this road, sweeping grass verges gave way to flowering gorse bushes and trees concealing the rest of the eight-foot-high wire-mesh fence. The marchers approached the open gates. There, in front of them, were the four women chained to the fence. Just behind them, through the gates, stood the sentry box where MOD guards were on their daily duty.

*Eunice*: Then the press and television came. The base Commander was there. And then lots of MOD police and, following them, the civil police. It was pandemonium. We heard the Commander say,

'Have you got the mug shots?'

More people started arriving and kissing us. Then the marchers came led by the Fallout Marching Band with our 'Women for Life on Earth' banner, and Thalia doing somersaults all the way. They all looked so beautiful with their scarves and ribbons and flowers. It was like a carnival. The colours, the beauty, the sun . . . and so many people!

On arrival the marchers delivered this letter to the base Commander.

### WOMEN'S ACTION FOR DISARMAMENT

### *Women for Life on Earth*

We are a group of women from all over Britain who have walked one hundred and twenty miles from Cardiff to deliver this letter to you. Some of us have brought our babies with us this entire distance. We fear for the future of all our children, and for the future of the living world which is the basis of all life.

We have undertaken this action because we believe that the nuclear arms race constitutes the greatest threat ever faced by the human race and our living planet. We have chosen Greenham Common as our destination because it is this base which our Government has chosen for 96 'Cruise' without our consent. The British people have never been consulted about our Government's nuclear defence policy. We know that the arrival of these hideous weapons at this base will place our entire country in the position of a front-line target in any confrontation between the two superpowers, Russia and the United States of America. We in Europe will not accept the sacrificial role offered us by our North Atlantic Treaty Organisation (NATO) allies. We will not be the victims in a war which is not of our making. We wish to be neither the initiators nor the targets of a nuclear holocaust. We have had enough of our military and political leaders who squander vast sums of money and human resources on weapons of mass destruction while we can hear in our hearts the millions of human beings throughout the world whose needs cry out to be met. We are implacably opposed to the siting of US Cruise Missiles in this country. We represent thousands of ordinary people who are opposed to these weapons and we will use all our resources to prevent the siting of these

16

missiles here. We want the arms race to be brought to a halt now – before it is too late to create a peaceful, stable world for our future generations.

Later the base Commander came out and looked disdainfully at everybody.

'As far as I'm concerned,' he said, 'you can stay here for as long as you like.'

He was dismissing women, and none of them was prepared to take that.

Later that day there was a rally. Women who had done nothing on their own for years were suddenly getting to their feet to speak out to the crowds about what we must do to halt the nuclear lunacy.

*Wendy Franklin, a potter, had come up from the Isle of Wight to join in the celebration:* I remember the women at that final rally and how they sensed their own power. They each clambered on to the trailer without notes or practice, to speak to the crowds. They reached out to us with their hearts surprising themselves and celebrating with us their new-found strength. We began to understand that the message of Greenham was, 'No one can do it for you, you have to do it for yourself.'

That evening people stayed to demonstrate their solidarity with the chained women. Permission was given to build a fire on a concrete slab. This fire became the focal point of the gathering and was later to become the heart of the camp. The weather was beautiful and that first night was spent in sleeping bags under the stars.

On Sunday more people came to visit bringing a frame tent, hot food, large containers of water and firewood. Above all, they brought encouragement. Every day more supplies arrived: chemical toilets, calor gas burners and blankets. There was great excitement when their first post was delivered – a telegram from Bradford Women's Liberation Group.

It was this practical and inspiring support from all over the country that kept the marchers at the gate. For three days they were able to have a rota of women chained to the fence. But by the end of the week, with all the local support, the marchers decided to establish a permanent picket. They called it a peace camp.

They also issued a challenge to the Government and the media,

17

demanding a public discussion on television with the Defence Secretary. The Government replied to this demand for a public debate by saying the matter of nuclear defence had been fully discussed. They backed their claim by listing five occasions when the subject had been debated in British universities!

At that stage relations with the men on the base were pleasant and polite. They even helped the marchers fix up a standpipe to the mains water supply on the road opposite the main gate. But their attitude began to change later when they realised that the march was only the beginning.

## 2
# A Different Lifestyle

The encampment at the main gate wasn't really called anything at first, it was just referred to as the Peace Camp. But one weekend, a woman who was visiting painted the immortal words 'Women's Peace Camp' on big pieces of board in green, white and violet letters (the suffragette colours representing the first letters of their demand: Give Women Votes!). It was all done in a flurry of creativity and energy. The boards were decorated with rich purple fruit and a white dove of peace. Everyone helped put them up on display to all the passing traffic.

Respect for the idea of a women's initiative, which had been stressed on the march, continued at the camp and affected the lifestyle of the women, and the few men and children living there. When the press came, it was women who spoke to them in a conscious effort to promote an image of women doing things in their own right and for their own reasons. It was a step towards countering the media's concentration on male personalities and male-oriented news.

The camp adopted routines that ensured women could speak and act for themselves. Chores were generally shared and everyone took turns at those tasks traditionally done by either men or women exclusively, though not without some disagreements.

As the news came filtering through with pictures and reports telling the outside world what was happening at the new Women's Peace Camp, it began to catch women's imaginations. New women began to arrive and with them came more support . . . and the beginnings of the media interest.

*Caroline Taylor arrived a few days after the marchers:* We were a mixed lot, and pretty naive when it came to using the media. Perhaps it was our naivety however, that struck a chord in so many people who rallied round to help and give us moral support. I remember the disgust one woman felt after a tabloid photographer had persuaded her, in an unguarded moment, to pose in front of the fence, wreathed in chains, hands clasped and face uplifted in meek supplication. The attitudes of such journalists probably hardened our resolve as much as anything; we eventually learned to refuse to be used in this way. We wanted to get the message across on our own terms.

It seemed fairly inevitable that we would not get our debate, and we wondered if we had hit a snag. Should we set ourselves a time limit? For most of September the weather was fine and warm but it obviously couldn't last. For a while some of us had a private agreement that we would pack up the week before the CND October rally, walk to London and call it a day. But support kept coming in the form of visits, presents and letters so that peace-camping became an end in itself, and our enthusiasm for it waxed rather than waned. Our arguments became more refined as we learned more. We all read books, many of us for the first time. We got more horrified at the extent of the arms race, and rapidly became more radical as our 'normal' lives receded and we immersed ourselves in full-time 'public relations' work to get across our views. The idea of 'giving up' became impossible. There were too many people behind us. Within a few weeks I was no longer going home for visits: Greenham was my home.

About three weeks after they arrived came the first gale, and some people stayed up all night holding down tents and looking after children. By that time the bright sunshine had given way to torrents of rain and a lot of time was spent trying to dry out bedding every day. The problem of encroaching mud was temporarily solved by putting down bracken.

Shortly after the gale, the first relatively solid structure arrived, a blue portakabin. It was used both for sleeping and as an office which was not a very satisfactory arrangement but a definite improvement. The portakabin involved a financial commitment of twenty pounds a week. Funding was offered by various trade unions and donations were arriving in every post.

The camp was undoubtedly getting established. While those living there were adjusting to the new lifestyle, getting themselves and their families used to the idea that it wasn't just a fairweather struggle, people elsewhere were working out how to help and spread the word about Greenham. It had already become a controversial development in the peace movement.

*Sarah Hopkins*: Many of us who felt as strongly and deeply as those at the camp were kept from that experience by distance, other people's needs, no money, doubts about ourselves and confusion about what is the right/useful/wise thing to do. Some of us couldn't imagine ever being in a position to drop everything and go like they seemed to have done. Some of us would have liked to, but not all of us. Most of us felt torn. The women at Greenham – they were brave, yes . . . but they were lucky too. We were attracted but at the same time scared of something that seemed so spectacular.

Those of us in CND were preoccupied with having good, fruitful meetings and getting our brave letters in the local paper. Did what was happening at Greenham put our efforts in the shade?

Greenham was put on the agenda at meetings and no one knew what to say about it. But you could be sure to hear:

'What I want to know is, why aren't they at home looking after their families . . .?'

'It seems to be mostly women, why's that?'

'Hadn't we better go and find out for ourselves?'

It felt scarey. There is disquiet when we are trying to decide what we dare commit ourselves to. Greenham made me feel awe, guilt, excitement, pride and envy – sometimes all at once!

But there was no doubt, the significance of the camp was seeping through. It was no ordinary bit of protest: it aroused lots of interest and anticipation. Campaigning was being redefined and we defended ourselves and our contribution.

'These are hard-bitten, radical people, I'm not like that so . . .'

'Well if that's what they want to do that's fine by me, but . . .'

'Well I just hope they get the publicity they deserve . . .'

'I don't see what they hope to achieve just by sitting there . . .'

'It gives the disarmament movement a bad image . . .'

Greenham had become the scapegoat for lots of our doubts. We were all vulnerable because it is so hard to see where you are going and what you are achieving as a pressure group.

Neither did it go down well in couples where the bloke couldn't see why on earth women should want to work primarily on their own. The discussions were often passionate but fruitless, Greenham was touching nerves that people didn't know they had. No one looked at the military and asked, 'Why men only?' and no one looked at Greenham and asked, 'Why not women?' People weren't curious, they were cross/confused.

Eventually we did go. It took a few hours to feel part of it, but that feeling has never gone. The idea of being a woman really thrilled me for the first time. We can do anything! . . . and we care about each other while we're doing it . . . it's like coming alive!

Recharged, we were able to go back to the group with our joy and our eye-witness account. We began collecting logs and clothes and money and arranging trips up to the camp. Us women were looking each other in the eye more, and we had a bit more to say for ourselves.

Messages were coming from the camp all the time. They needed more people. Most of the original marchers had gone back home to carry on their work locally, but not all of them.

*Barbara Doris is a pensioner living in Wales. She had been on the march and stayed at the camp for a while:* I am a retired science teacher and I became very worried about the effects of radiation on all forms of life.

I remember when I was 17. We went through the blitz in Liverpool after a long time of severe unemployment. I could see unemployment rising again in the 1980s and I thought 'last time it was stopped by war – not again!

It was my war memories that kept me there. Nothing else seemed worth doing while the threat of annihilation was so real. We could see that our camp was encouraging other folk to do something and that made me stay too, despite weeks of hardship under canvas and lots at home to draw me back.

Some nights we wondered if it was all worth it when there was only three of us there, sitting round the fire. It got very thin on the ground at times. But it survived because when some of us needed to go away and think again, or we wanted to go back home, there always seemed to be just enough new ones ready to move in.

By November the peace camp was firmly established. Everyone was getting organised for the winter.

A small village was slowly sprouting up on the common, outside the main gate. More caravans appeared, some gaily painted with slogans and the names of groups who'd donated them: 'Arms are for linking' and 'Dorset Peace Council'. There were tipis and tents and elsan toilet tents. Visitors brought banners and we made our own, to line the edge of the highway and the entrance to the main gate.

An enormous structure of polythene, tarpaulin and branches was built as a communal area. Just inside the doorway was a cauldron hanging from a wooden tripod over the ever-smoking fire surrounded by orange boxes and camping chairs. At the back of the structure there was an opening to the kitchen caravan; along the wall was a large table with leaflets, badges, photos and donated flowers. A noticeboard displayed letters, messages and posters advertising events. In one corner was a stack of material, old sheets and paint for making banners . . . and wool for weaving webs.

Local people offered the use of their baths and telephones. Daily chores such as fetching water, answering mail and washing dishes took longer as the weather grew colder. There was also lots to do in the new 'office'. Typewriters, donated stationery and a duplicator made it possible to keep the media informed, organise actions and make links with the people in the groups who were offering help.

*Caroline*: Every Sunday we invited one or two people to come and talk to a public meeting. The first two gatherings we organised in this way were quite big – about 200 people, some of them motivated by curiosity and unconvinced, which was what we wanted. Joan Ruddock, Chairperson of national CND, came one filthy wet night, which gave us a big lift. It was the first hint of CND approval, and although some of us felt that CND had dragged its heels in acknowledging our credibility we still wanted their help.

While we became increasingly in demand to talk to groups and improved our handling of the media, the men for the most part were happy to do an ample share of the menial tasks and stay in the background. Many of us trusted and liked the men and appreciated their support. My letters home at that time were full of community spirit and affection between us all.

One day a regular visitor to the camp came to tell us about the CND Conference he had just been to in Coventry. When the peace camp had been mentioned, the whole conference stood up and applauded. This brought lumps to our throats despite our concern that we shouldn't be seen as extraordinary.

In those early months the camp was seen as a new initiative in the peace movement. Its sheer presence was visible evidence that opposition to Cruise was serious. It was acting out our beliefs in a way that influenced others.

*Sarah Green worked with mentally disturbed people in Sheffield and after visiting the camp she decided to give up her job to move here:* We're here every day reminding people that the men in there are building silos while the American military force is getting their nuclear weapons ready to put in them. The people going in and out of the base can't forget that there are objections to what they're doing. They have to question themselves a little bit just because we're here. Every day hundreds of people pass along the main road. They probably have nothing to do with the controversy over nuclear weapons but we hope it makes them think, 'What's going on in there that makes women live at the gate and give up their normal lives?'

Getting people to think about the issue is as important as providing a focus for those already committed to it. It was a focus where people could join together to consolidate the ideas and organise action. It was later to become specifically a women's meeting place. The camp also played a vital role in highlighting the Cruise decision. The style of this kind of action attracted the media. The camp made Cruise newsworthy.

It inspired some people to look for new ways of making their political voices heard. Voting is not sufficient, we have to take more direct and personal responsibility. We have to take action.

*Shushu Al-Sabbagh had recently finished school and was preparing for university, but after hearing a woman from the camp speaking at a* CND *conference she decided it was more important for her to move to Greenham:* I don't see this situation being resolved by parliamentary means . . . maybe if there's enough extra-parliamentary pressure we could do it that way but there's more to it. I don't think disarmament is one little thing that you can achieve without other bits of society changing. You won't achieve disarmament unless you remove the desire and need for men to fight . . . I think the future rests on women.

There cannot be fundamental political change without personal change. We have to demystify experience by trying new things in order to gain confidence. We have to find a new identity so that we are not defined in terms of our family roles. We also need to cross

24

all the barriers that have traditionally divided women – we need to deepen our bonds with each other because we need each other emotionally and politically.

Somehow we had to try to translate our idealism into our life at the camp. Our way of living and working together had to be consistent with our overall aims. New ways of doing things had to be found and this wasn't easy.

We went because we do not agree with the power imbalance in our world between rich and poor, men and women, black and white, old and young. We are still here to say that, but we also have to construct an alternative.

In some ways a peace camp is the ideal, as well as the obvious place to begin finding/changing/preparing ourselves. In other ways the pressures, living conditions and constant change of faces prevent things being properly and carefully worked through. People lack the time and energy to challenge each other's behaviour and control their own haste and impulses.

*Barbara D*: The hardest part was coping with each other and trying to form a community that didn't fall into the ways we were used to – that was our biggest task.

There was the almost inevitable impatience on the part of one or two to do things without discussion, and so they became leaders and lots of the others had a tendency to fall in behind them. So we had, outside the base fence, a set-up like the one inside and like the one that had set up the base, a microcosm of our patriarchal culture. With this went an immaturity on the part of many of the campers which showed itself in wastefulness and thoughtlessness for others and some violent talk. This drove me away after two months.

Despite wanting to include everybody there was no efficient democratic decision-making process set up to ensure that this happened. It is perhaps inevitable that people who are centrally involved in the camp and have stayed there for many months end up taking leadership roles, though often they are created by the expectation of others.

*Shushu*: It is a problem. We try to work it out so that when women commit themselves fully to moving here and making it their home, sharing knowledge with them is a priority. We have to give lots of time to that. It is important because otherwise you make yourself indispensable and that hampers you and the camp.

*Ruth Nichol is a teacher/explorer/acrobat/community arts worker:*
My very first visit to Greenham was on 5 December 1981. I'll never
forget arriving in the dark in a transit van with the Sheffield
Women's Peace Group to 'deliver' Sarah and the tipi and set her up
to live there. All expectant we were. Excited by her decision to
move to this faraway place and leave us all behind, and curious to
find out what it was like.

Oh horrors! Exhausted from the long cramped journey, we
slowly tumbled out to stretch our legs only to discover men already
beginning to untie the ropes which held the tipi poles on the roof.
We protested, surprised at their presumptuousness. Women came
over to see what was the matter, one saying, 'We're not like that
here, we don't separate into groups, we're all learning to do things
together as equals.' We were all a bit numb from the journey and
now quite speechless with incredulity and anger that a Women's
Peace Camp would not give us room to make our own decisions.
Someone did manage to explain that we would do things our way
when we wanted to and we didn't like having parts of our lives taken
away from us. One woman then came up and told us heartily where
to put our tipi. We felt like crawling back into the van together and
staying there.

Eventually we got the tipi set up as Sarah wanted it and we spent
that night sleeping off the rather depressing events of the evening,
hoping things would change with the dawn.

Breakfast-time next day we made tentative sorties to the camp
fire by the main gate to try to get to know people a bit better. I
remember one bloke sounding forth about women being sexist and
hateful, and at least two women were giving away a lot of energy
explaining to him what it was really about. We went wood gathering
across the road to help the general wood pile and to start a fire off in
Sarah's tipi.

I think we lit a fire that afternoon. What I do remember was the
white light ritual that Veronica started off in the tipi – sitting in a
circle holding hands, humming and aahing and imagining light rising
out of each one of us into the air above our heads and then 'sitting'
over the tipi to keep Sarah safe. While we were humming a woman
came in and joined the circle. That was Jayne. It felt like the ritual
had begun its work, Jayne was there so it was OK. We could 'leave'
Sarah safely.

26

# 3
# A Place of Our Own

*Shushu*: On 21 December we woke up to find that a section of rough land next to the camp had been bulldozed flat ready to receive sewer pipes being laid by a local firm. The pipes were meant to go through the middle of the camp and into the base to update the sewage system and accommodate 1,200 more US soldiers.

We were politely asked to move one caravan and one tipi. We explained that we could not allow them to continue work which supports the Death Machine. Then we sat down in front of their digger and stopped their work.

Once we'd told them why we were taking action and that we felt absolutely no hostility towards them, they seemed very sympathetic and friendly. One of the women spoke to the Commander at the base, expressing our determination to prevent the pipes being laid.

The digger withdrew to the other side of the road and the workers left without incident. The message was clear – we are prepared to act, we are serious, we will stop you . . . the pipes will not be laid.

We learned several things from all this . . . first of all, that we need to be up early in the morning! We were forced to think out our attitudes to confrontation . . . we never know when we'll have to deal with it again.

As well as showing what we are against, we must show what we are for. Life-affirming actions are important too.

*Sarah G*: On New Year's Eve five of us walked around the base, following the nine miles of fence widdershins (anti-clockwise). Our motivation was our love for life and a celebration at the turning of the seasons and the returning of a new year.

We called in celebration to the trees and the Earth, and hung painted and written messages along the fence. Some of them got hung in almost inaccessible muddy places, not for vast numbers of people but for ourselves or other peace campers to see. Sometimes a message would be left for a single house or a place of work inside the base.

I felt that the messages were like presents, gifts of a wise word or a beautiful image. At one point we passed a garden swing and hung on it 'DARE TO HOPE, DARE TO GIVE, DARE TO DREAM' and a star.

It felt very good encircling the base but I wondered what I was doing following such an unnatural boundary. I remembered my uncertainty about whether to put my attention into understanding the anti-life forces of violence and destruction or to put my attention into valuing life and being part of a creative life spirit.

A day and a night later, I was lying in my tipi and things began to make sense. I remembered something someone had told me about a community in Africa . . . how it deals with one of its clan who has done something antisocial . . . against the code of the people.

The person is surrounded by all the others in the community. Each of the people remembers good things about the person, things about who they are and what they have done, right back to their birth. They make their statements of support and recognition. This goes on until the person in the centre gets enough affirmation and good feelings, until they believe in themselves and Life and no longer need to damage. Surrounding the base with our calling and messages of love of Life reminds me of the community surrounding the antisocial individual.

We must talk to the men building the silos and we must talk to the men in power, through the media. I believe that the people who are creating the missile programme are basically the same as us . . . They are not full of sin . . . but they are out of contact with Life. They have become detached and inhuman and are asking for attention.


By now, people outside the camp were convinced that what we were doing was positive and purposeful. This helped us through our difficult patches and enabled us to look beyond our internal wrangles.

Regular newsletters were being printed by the Women's Peace Camp and South Oxfordshire Peace Campaign. The ideas were spreading, a new peace camp was set up at Molesworth, the proposed site for another 64 American Cruise missiles, on 28 December 1981.

*Jayne*: . . . a group of people gathered outside the main gates of RAF Molesworth. They took with them two caravans. A fireplace was made and the first of many fires was kindled. Some people began digging away patches of snow to put up tents. The weather was misty and very cold . . . the atmosphere was happy and optimistic. People sang and the Bishop came and gave a service. Ten of us from Greenham Common Women's Peace Camp were there. This was a very important, exciting day for us . . . the escalation of peace camps at military bases had begun . . .

Back at Greenham a letter arrived which confirmed that we had taken possession of the Council land at the entrance to the base.

NEWBURY DISTRICT COUNCIL

20 January 1982

Dear Mrs John,

I refer to the meeting which took place this morning when you and two other representatives of the Peace Camp discussed the Camp's occupation of part of Greenham Common . . . During that meeting you were handed a press release giving details of the decision taken by the Recreation and Amenities Committee at its meeting last night and you were also asked if you would now be prepared peaceably to give up possession of the Council's land and remove your encampment. You indicated that you would not be prepared to do so and that you would obstruct any moves by the Council to remove you.

. . . I am naturally disappointed by your reaction this morning and am therefore writing to ask you to reconsider your decision and formally to request you to secure the removal of the encampment within 14 days of the date of this letter.

. . . May I remind you that, whilst the Council does not wish to be forced into taking court proceedings against the persons at the encampment, the Committee has authorised the taking of such action if you are not prepared to remove the encampment.

Please ensure that the contents of this letter are brought to the attention of all persons who are at present at the encampment or who may subsequently join it.

Yours sincerely,

W. J. Turner

Director of Legal and Administrative Services

The Women's Peace Camp,
RAF Greenham Common

*To the Newbury District Councillors*

They used to burn witches and the law of the time endorsed it. At one time it was illegal for a married woman to retain her property. The Law is not a creature which exists independently. Laws have been wrong and they have been changed. When laws clash with the developing moral standards of the time then these laws are put aside – ignored. Human beings make, break, change laws and ignore laws that are morally wrong.

If the Women's Peace Camp is destroyed due to part of a law (a very old one, I believe 1925?) then the people who try to endorse such a law, who go against morality in this way by trying to remove the women at the camp, they, YOU are responsible for that action. Don't blindly obey laws that go against Truth and Life – simply ignore them – just as wrong laws have been ignored in the past and eventually changed.

The people who try to move the women at the camp must not hide behind hindering laws – and must not let themselves be pressurised into enforcing them . . . Nature is in the balance. Certain sections of our society have the power to actually destroy the Earth – our home. We at the peace camp seek to alter this suicidal course. We see the realities of the situation and must try to stop this senseless state of affairs.

The protection of life on this planet goes beyond the Law and politics. To overcome the confusions of Law and politics takes only two things – common sense and the ability to see the truth (reality) behind the actions of human beings.

The problem of nuclear disarmament and the protection of life is a nationwide/worldwide problem and it is not the place of a small local council to allow itself to be a pawn in the dangerous military game.

There was no reply.


Luckily we don't need the authorities to keep us on our toes. We don't depend on their reactions for our impetus, we use our own initiative, energy and ideas. Around that time there was lots of talk

30

about having an Equinox Festival on 21 March followed by a blockade of the base on the Monday.

We were trying to stop Cruise missiles coming to Greenham, so the preparations for their arrival had to be hindered and disrupted. By obstructing the workers and supplies from entering the base we could achieve this. It sparked off much soul-searching about non-violence and the tactic of women-only actions which had already been raised by the threat of eviction. One of the fears was that men may more readily respond with violence because of their conditioning and because of feeling protective towards women in a dangerous situation. That would take away women's responsibility for their own actions. It was also felt that the police may respond in a more heavy-handed way to the men participating in an action. Some thought the police would feel uncomfortable and be less competent when faced with peaceful resistance from hundreds of cheerful, smiling, singing women, particularly as their training relates to mixed, uncontrollable, aggressive crowds.

There was a further compliction in this first attempt to involve a lot of people in the direct action of a blockade. For the first time women at Greenham were finding themselves with the responsibility of calling people to take part in arrestable offences. With no previous experience of big actions it was an unpredictable situation for everybody.

*Caroline*: The blockade had caught the imagination of most of us, but the festival was seen by some as peripheral and irrelevant. The theory behind it was to bring together various creative growing points in our culture – the Women's, the Green and New Age Movements, religion, art and music – to demonstrate the value of each to each. By inviting various artists, dancers, etc. to participate we hoped to raise their political consciousness and give a feeling of common direction. The point didn't come across to everybody. Some people thought the divisions arbitrary and disliked the flavour of it. The fact that I was working closely with men to arrange it all, publicise it and so on, was also disliked.

In the midst of it all, while I was in London for a couple of days, two of the men at the camp were arrested for painting designs on one of the gates to the base. The women were alarmed and the following day decided that the men were a liability and would have to leave. I felt the decision to be a betrayal, and the rift in the camp widened.

31

*Jayne*: From the beginning of the camp there had been terrific scenes over the women-only/mixed thing.

Over the first few months many women came and left very quickly when they realised that men were living there. I used to think, 'Oh why don't you stay and try to make it how you want it?' But it was all part of the process and the women-only aspect took a while to take shape in our minds.

Personally, I didn't realise for quite a while that the camp had to be women-only. Then it suddenly sank in and it became obvious that it was the right thing to do. The next two months were very difficult. The decision nearly got reversed, but just didn't. A few of us were putting everything we had into upholding that first decision. But it was painful because we were such a mixture and we couldn't do it without hurting each other.

*Sarah G*: When we had our first women-only meeting it was unanimous that we wanted the camp and the actions to be women only . . . but we didn't think of the practicalities. We got carried away with the idea that this was what we wanted to do. Someone said at the end of the meeting, 'We can't just leave now, how are we going to do this?' And there was a feeling that it would just somehow get done. Then we were back in the tent for a coffee break and all the men were going, 'Well, what happened?', 'What came out of the meeting?' There was an awkward silence. It was important that no one was seen as the leader, otherwise they'd all pick on her. One of us scribbled a group statement and read it out aloud. '. . . only women live here and stay overnight – men welcome to visit during the day.' Everyone sort of gasped and all hell was let loose. The men went completely mad. Their worst elements came out. There was one bloke staying here for a couple of days who had come specifically to give us a workshop on self-control. Well he just couldn't take it – he bashed into this cauldron of boiling water, almost spilling it all over one of the women, and then he just stormed off. Someone else was going wild saying, 'I built this structure' and he picked up an axe and started to chop down the tarpaulin.

We hadn't meant it to happen like that. We knew what we wanted but hadn't worked out how to do it and then it all came out like a shock. We tried to calm it all down saying , 'It's not quite as it seems . . .', 'We thought you might like to move down to the Green Gate . . . we'll help you move your stuff . . .' and they kept saying,

'We're never leaving, we're not going to go.'

Half an hour later they had got their tipi on top of the van and they were off to London.

*Sarah H*: Inside and outside the camp – uproar. This reaction didn't make it any easier for those of us struggling away in CND groups to get moral and financial support for the camp. Should we try and make light of their decision and encourage people to see it as nothing bigger than a temporary, tactical move? Or should we go into all the headache that had surrounded the role of men at the camp and risk people's outrage and disassociation? We listened to what each other had to say. We argued. We said, eventually we have all got to learn to live together and we're not going to learn how to do that by going off and doing things separately. We said if working to stop Cruise means you can't co-operate with men then how will the next generation be produced to make it all worthwhile? We said we didn't like women-only groups . . . it's women's faults if they let men dominate . . . it's wrong to blame men for the nuclear mess we're in . . . how can we expect more sympathetic men to support us if we just tell them to go away? We said women have every right to organise on their own around their own demands. We said women don't want men's comments and certainly not their approval – it's irrelevant! We said it'll do men good – see how they like women's work 24 hours a day every day. We said we want to achieve something for ourselves by ourselves. If men are at the camp it will be assumed they did it all.

There was rage, bewilderment and tension. Something that should have gone in women's favour, was actually dividing us. Our working relationship was being shaken because there was no way to compromise on this. Interesting difficulties arose. If men weren't very welcome at the camp, how were we going to get stuff there? After all, who were the drivers, who had the car keys? How many women could go to Greenham now without feeling that they were betraying their partners? Would men who felt hurt be prepared to support us at all?

The reaction was totally out of proportion to the event. It stirred up lots of secret longings in women and that was met with fear.

However, no one had suggested, 'Thou shalt never speak to men again', or 'All men in the peace movement are to be suspected of foul play until further notice from the women at Greenham'.

It was we who made it a scandal because it questioned the way men and women interacted. What should we as women, do? What could we do with so many responsibilities and people depending on us already? If only we had room in our lives to be just ourselves! Has anybody noticed all the realms of life that are closed to women by custom, assumption, the possibility of violent attack?

We went to Greenham. We needed to talk to them about it. I remember sitting round the campfire in the huge woman-made polythene marquee that housed about 50 of us very comfortably. We went around in a circle and everyone took a turn to say what they felt about the women-only thing. I'm a bit talkative and dominant and going round in a circle so I couldn't butt in was a stunning experience. It was the first time I really listened properly to women and wished every one of them had said more. I realised that I hadn't spent listening time preparing my speech! One woman was nervous – it seemed unfair, she said, that all the men who had changed their lives to enable the women to stay at the camp should now not be able to bring the kids down and stay at weekends. Traditional living patterns were being disrupted. We were rejecting the very people who had given us most support. I could see what a tearing apart it was. It was the wrong decision for her, there was no doubt about that, and she and others decided to leave after the March Festival.

But it was still absolutely right for the camp and for many other women there as well as lots of us watching their every move. It was right because all they were saying was, 'We want to do this by ourselves for an assortment of reasons and we believe it is the right way for this camp to run and develop.' They were saying they wanted to live and work together unhindered and unquestioned on half an acre of land. The rest of the world is a free for all. That's what I mean about the response being over the top.

The women-only decision came at that time partly as a response to the threat of eviction and the coming blockade, but also from a gut feeling about the need for women to work together.

By now some of the bad feelings about the women-only decision have softened. In retrospect, some of the women who left at that time now say it was probably the right decision but it was done in a hurtful way. Maybe that is so. Maybe it happened like that because we are having to sort things out quickly and we are not always the people we would like to be.

With the blockade coming immediately after the Festival, and our imminent eviction from the common land controlled by Newbury District Council, the camp was becoming a hive of activity.

National and international media were descending in force, trying to isolate spokespeople who would provide them with one-liners to define the camp and the women protesting.

All of this caused disagreements between women. It was a dilemma. We wanted the camp to get as much publicity as possible but many women were uncomfortable and unconfident in front of the camera. We didn't want to abandon our principles and play to the notion of leaders for the sake of publicity, but it is hard to change old patterns of domination and control. The media seemed to have the upper hand, and we needed to have them on our side. So individual women stepped forward and became 'leaders'. There were many arguments and accusations. We are looking for new ways of working, not for power over others. This is a problem which still continues and women still put themselves forward as leaders while others shut off and allow this to happen. But there are hopeful signs that some of the press are beginning to understand these different ways of working, and we are learning to confront each other when old patterns emerge.

While we were dealing with this media invasion, we were also organising workshops in preparation for the coming blockade, and arrangements for the Festival were being finalised.

21 March arrived. Although the day began with drizzling rain it burst into life as thousands of people gathered to celebrate and rejoice in the Festival for Life. On the next day the first blockade took place. This was the first time women at Greenham put non-violence to the test on a large scale. It was also the first time there was a concerted effort to disrupt the workings of the base. This action drew a large number of women to Greenham, some of whom moved to the camp and others became active supporters.

## 4
# Talking Through Non-Violence

During the March action we made a public commitment to non-violence. As a tactic, it is definitely appropriate to our needs, here and now, in this phase of our protest. That is not to say we condemn all those who use violent resistance. We are not living in El Salvador, Northern Ireland or Soweto exposed to the brutal intimidation and exploitation of our own or foreign governments. Most of us are not victims of the violence of material deprivation but for many of us the fears we live with are as debilitating and painful. Nuclear nightmares, fear of the streets at night, emotional deprivation and isolation in a nuclearised society are as real and frightening as a loaded gun in your back or not knowing when you will eat again. The path to madness is littered with victims and a different kind of madness rules us from above. The peace we are seeking is both material and psychological. We are trying to create awareness of the crisis in order to avert it and promote re-examination of the principles upon which the solution of crises are determined.

Talking through non-violence is an obvious and essential part of our work. We cannot express a collective view on it because for everyone it is a different experience and has different political and personal implications. We all think it is the right way for us to go about things, but that doesn't make it easy, or mean that we are always satisfied with the results of our non-violent direct action.

Some of us have chosen non-violence as a strategy because of its practical advantages to us. After all, we cannot match the resources that could be used against us and our non-violence makes it difficult for the forces of law and order to legitimise any mistreatment, especially when the world is watching. Some of us have chosen non-violence as a philosophy of life, a principle on which to base all our behaviour not just our political campaign. This comes from a belief that violence breeds violence and damages those who resort to it. Means and ends have to be consistent. Martin Luther King likened revolution to a seed, and the society that grows from it he saw as a tree. If the seed does not embody all the essential goodness needed to produce the best possible results, the tree cannot flourish. Gandhi drew a clear distinction between the short and long-term gains of resistance. He said the good done by violence is temporary, but the evil it does is permanent. You can never mend broken heads or broken hearts.

It would be impossible to reflect all the views on non-violence at the camp. There is an abundance of convictions and doubts and these are some of the questions we keep asking ourselves: What can non-violence realistically achieve? What do we do with our anger? What if you were raped? Is damage to property violent? How can I stop feeling violent when I see it all around me? Haven't I the right to save myself by any means? Can you expect a peaceful society to emerge from violent struggle?

At present a great deal will have to be left unsaid and unresolved because that's the way it is. But a few perspectives can be heard through the voices of women at Greenham.

*Gillian Booth*: Those who stand up against violence should be honest about their own violence and their struggle with it. In that way we, I, can be seen as ordinary and human like everyone else, but with a firm resolve to heal and stop the things within me that damage me and hurt people I love, because it is with people I love that I am most likely to feel the need to hurt.

When a bomb is dropped killing 80,000 people and you are told at three years old that it was a good thing because it brought peace, what can you do but set your jaw and clench your thin, already stressed little body against such contradiction, especially if to question would mean more ridicule and more denial that there was anything wrong, only something wrong with you?

So I learned to block and block myself from my anger and tried to be a good little girl and then maybe the harassment and the belittling would stop. The child psychologist I was eventually recommended to suggested to my mother that such damage might take four generations to resolve. I felt my body set into a great resolve: that if I ever had children, I would not pass it on. That the responsibility to stop it lay with me. I was seven years old.

My mother gave me a book about the extermination camp at Belsen to read. There were photographs of floating bodies, accounts of experimental gynaecology, all sorts of horrors. She said, 'Read this'. She might just as well have said also, 'so that you will learn to hate'. But I think that my mother liked what she read in that book, and I knew at 12 that she hated Germans much more than she liked Jews, but that she hated Jews too. No, it was herself and her own brutality and abusiveness she hated, and if she had been able to talk about it, she could have healed herself. Years later I found my rage at this, her parental irresponsibility, but then I just knew that what she was doing was wrong because of so many things, but mostly because she gave me books to read about torture when I was beginning to feel my sexuality.

When I was 19, after several abusive relationships with young men (and one good one) I married to get away from home. In 1961 there appeared to be few options. I didn't think of myself as violent but what I didn't realise was that my jaw, which had started to make strange clicking noises when I was 16, had begun to dislocate from the pressure I was putting on it, clamping down to stop myself from screaming. My marriage was not a happy one. My husband invalidated and belittled me, and I played games to get back at him. Again, years later in therapy I realised I had married someone very much like my mother. When I was 23, my first daughter was born and 19 months later, the second. They are 16 and nearly 18 now. One day after screaming at them I sat down, crying with guilt and shame, and remembered what the psychologist had said. I knew that if I did not leave their father and start to heal myself I would start hurting them and I could not bear the thought. I was in America at the time; he was on a two-year work contract. Already I had become involved with the anti-Vietnam war movement and feminism and was in therapy and beginning to put pieces together. He was very threatened by my political and personal changes and didn't want to consider either living in the States so that we could share custody or living back in England with me having custody. All I knew was that if I went back to England under such circumstances I would end up really hurting myself: suicide. And hassling them, too. So in 1972 he came back here and I stayed there.

Today is two years to the day that I finally left America and came back to live in England with my lover, Arlene. We had been lovers for a year and friends for ten years. We left a trail of battles and skirmishes across America and brought them to England, for it was with her that I finally came to my full understanding and expression of all the pent-up violence. I could not believe the fights we had, could not believe that I had actually done what I did. It was the most passionate and involved relationship of my life and it brought up responses I didn't even know I had, and scared me. This violence came with us when we arrived at the camp 16 months ago. It was something neither of us liked. As for me: I was open about it, because I felt and feel now that if there is one place on the globe where I might be healed, where I could be honest about myself, this could be it.

Arlene and I are not together anymore; she found peace with Sarah. I'm crying now because it still hurts, that things had to be the way they were. I have no regrets, no resentment, no bitterness, only a deep sadness somewhere that I trust time will heal. I loved her more than any other human being (apart from my daughters) and I was more violent with her than with any other human being. Love and violence, love and violence.

Maybe I'll never lose the urge to hurt that comes sometimes in fraught situations. As long as I don't act on it, that's all that matters. But it would be nice not to have those feelings at all. Maybe in the next generation. Whatever. I broke the chain in this one.


*Rebecca Johnson*: I don't see non-violence as just a tactic. It is part of the accepted lie that violence is more powerful than non-violence and that people can somehow save themselves from violence by taking up arms. Thus non-violence is viewed as less valid, less desperate – a sort of liberal pastime, to be abandoned when the serious struggle begins.

I think this is wrong, but I also think that where the desperately oppressed choose arms they need to be supported, not judged. Yet I am afraid. We accept too easily the idea that violence is a more serious form of resistance.

When a non-violent protester is killed, people are quick to give up and say I told you so. That proves that non-violence fails. Thousands are killed in violent struggle, but few voices dare say that these deaths prove that violence has failed.

Revolutionary non-violence doesn't presume that the police, the army, the armed state will suddenly be transformed into benevolent supporters, their guns turning into flowers in their hands. They are trained and conditioned with violence and for a long time will continue to resort to it.

Yet history shows that violence and war are abject, miserable failures, incapable of solving or resolving any conflict. Wars come to an end when the participants are destroyed or too exhausted to continue. The conditions of that ending (I will not call it peace) fester and grow, become poisoned and distorted and may break out in localised wars as the whole system reconstructs and rearms, so that the Big War can be continued. That interim period is a breathing space so that the fighters can build up their resources and return more brutally.

We can't disinvent nuclear weapons, so we must evolve the moral and political attributes to render them useless. We have the capability of non-violence. The question is, have we the intelligence and courage to develop and trust it? And give it time? The dinosaurs failed to adapt to changing conditions and look what happened to them!

*Barbara H*: You are living in Northern Ireland, a child of say ten, and the pattern of your life is characterised by sniper gunshots and heavily armed paramilitary troops in reinforced vehicles patrolling the streets. Your urban surroundings reflect a grey, decaying patchwork of bullet-pocked brick and mortar, and the only relief is at the butt end of a row of houses where graffitists have stealthily painted a vivid image of a dove with a gun clasped in its feet.

After continually witnessing the brutality of war you will be deeply scarred. The psychological effects are long term and possibly permanent as both observers and participants become dehumanised. They have to – they couldn't survive without hardening themselves to those 'weaker' than themselves.

Northern Ireland is where children have learnt to hate and fear troops on the streets, and where wife-battering has the highest rate in the UK or Southern Ireland. With such effects, how can the ends justify the means?

(We look more closely at Northern Ireland in Chapter 14.)

We espouse the principle of non-violence and yet we cut fences. Is this not a form of violence?

*Rebecca*: At first I thought the division between violence and non-violence was easily identifiable. Violence hurts or injures, so you don't do it if you believe in non-violence. I felt good that we decided not to cut the fence on New Year's Day. But during that time we have talked and thought a lot about it and I began to realise it wasn't that simple.

Cutting the wire and taking down the fence is damage to property. Is that violence? Where do you draw the line? A carpenter takes a piece of wood and cuts and planes and shapes it into something else: a house, a bed or a child's toy. The wood is cut, but we don't call that violence. We do this all the time: cutting wheat to make bread, melting metal to reshape it, burning wood on our camp fire.

We are transforming things for other purposes. That's what creativity is about. Look at the high wire fence surrounding the base, topped by rolls of spiked barbed wire. What use is that? It encloses and 'protects' the nuclear base, with its reinforced concrete silos. It shuts people out of the common land that once was ours, purple with heather and thick with elderberry and rowan trees. Now razed flat and bare, scarred with runways. With our own hands we pull down the fence, making a huge door in the base. Only a few people can climb up a ladder and over the barbed wire, but thousands of common people can walk into the base through the door we have made into the common land.

Where is the violence? That whole fence and its purpose is violence, against us and against the land. Cutting the fence and making a door is part of our creativity, and as long as we take full responsibility for it, and for ensuring that no living creature is injured by our actions, then such transformation (like painting planes and runways with flowers and women's symbols) cannot be violent.


Non-violence as a strategy for the peace movement makes sense in terms of our aims, our need to grow in numbers and our need to be able to return again and again to challenge our oppressors and continue our work until it is no longer necessary. To this end the analysis now emerging from discussion amongst feminists is crucial to the peace movement's struggle. We can't possibly have peace in a world where inequalities exist. The struggle of the women's liberation movement is central to our task and aims. We're all in this together.

# 5
# Spontaneous Disruption

Our first major action was over and as the chill winds of March abated the spring brought warmer weather. Our spirits lifted with the temperature but this was overshadowed by the Council's threat of eviction. We had no warning of when it would happen.

*Ruth*: The March blockade had made a strong impression on me of the tangibility of our power as womyn when we are together, and I was curious to see how the womyn's peace camp was at a relatively quiet time. I stopped off to see Sarah at the camp on my way to a camping/cycling holiday.

Sarah came running across the drive to meet me all excited. 'We're building a tree house round that poplar tree on top of the big communal structure. It's supported by the structure so when the bailiffs come to try to destroy it, some of us will rush up into the tree house and say, "You bulldoze the structure down and you'll have our lives on your hands." We want to save the structure from being evicted.'

I put my bike down in the safety of her tipi and went for a walk along the fence with Sarah. As we talked, all the while we were looking for trees the base had been chopping down for no apparent reason, which Sarah said we could use in the building work. Before tea, which was cooking inside the structure, I climbed up the ladder to look at how the 'foundations' for the floor of the tree house worked. Sarah said an architect, Fiona, had been at the camp when they first got the idea, and she had convinced them that it was possible to do it without banging nails into the tree. I was fascinated, and said I'd like to help the next day.

That was the end of my holiday 'away from it all' and the beginning of one of the most exciting weeks of my life. We went gathering reeds from the side of the River Kennet to weave into walls and roof for the tree house – me, Jayne, Sarah, Io and Babs –

42

and as we hummed and sang and called out to each other, I felt a strange connecting timelessness – imagining women doing this together centuries ago and still doing it now all over the world wherever there is relative peace.

The actual weaving of the rushes was hilarious. We all developed our own ways of doing it with string 'stitches' – no one knew how it 'should' be done, so it was a beautiful creative work of art. This was my first experience of one important characteristic of Greenham – that things can be created as and when they are needed – it's both an organic and a political process: a response to whatever 'comes up' both in relation to what those in power do and to our needs as women.

From that time on there were spot blockades. Sometimes men going to work on the silos were faced with women blocking their way and they had to be re-routed, or women suddenly appeared when officials were expected, to remind the American military that there was great opposition to their use of Britain as a launch pad for Cruise missiles.

Spontaneity ensured that these acts of non-co-operation and disruption were not pre-empted by the authorities. There is enough flexibility at the peace camp to see that those who do the actions decide what tactics they want to use. We don't have the kind of strategy that mirrors the military institutions we oppose. We are not interested in handing out instructions or plans to people who have not been able to participate in the evolution of those plans. We want to work together, not boss each other about.

*Shushu*: We can't make long-term plans because we're in a precarious situation. It also depends on the people who are here. Someone will have an idea and it will be rejected or acted upon. We can be spontaneous. Like the flying blockade on 25 March. No one would have thought of that the week before. General Lew Allen, USAF Chief of Staff, was doing a little tour of bases in Britain to check on the work being done for Cruise. Some say it's behind schedule, and he had to come over to see for himself. We read about the visit in the *Guardian* the day before, and thought it would be a good idea to demonstrate very definitely to him and the public that we were indeed determined to keep the work behind schedule. So the night before, we rang up Alison at national CND and asked her to put out press releases. In the morning we went up to the works entrance and sat across it so the work force couldn't get in. Because it was a surprise, they were totally confused and didn't know what to do about it. Two workers stepped over us and through a little gap in the barbed wire but the rest stood around wondering . . .

The MOD police arrived and were also confused. They had very little communication with us. They didn't even ask us to move. Some workmen got angry because they said we were stopping them earning their wage to support their families. We talked to some of them while they were waiting, about whether work that could lead to people's death should be allowed to go on. But to get the message across in this kind of economic climate is hard. Jobs are scarce, we understand their fear of losing them.

The civil police eventually came up for a look at us and then drove away again. The MOD police and foreman came out and told the workers to back down and go to another gate to get in.

Having forced the workers to divert to another gate, and left a web over the gateway, everyone moved back to the ongoing blockade at the main gate. Base personnel and police were totally bewildered. They did not even ask any women to move. One inspector did approach, to ask if we had decided when it was going to finish. However, that decision was taken out of our hands. At about 4.30 p.m. an American serviceman tried to break through. He was furiously revving his bike, trying to psyche up the women blocking his way and suddenly, the bike burst into flames between his legs. He wasn't seriously hurt, but everyone scattered for fear of the fire. Then control of the base was formally handed back to the MOD . . . until next time.

Later on an effective 15-day blockade was maintained which stopped all traffic going in the main gate to the base. *Mandy Bush was one of the women on this blockade. She had moved from London to live at the camp and has kept a diary of her experiences here:*

*20 May, Thursday.* 15th day of blockade at main gate.

A soggy morning . . . rain ran down the road under the polythene, soaking mattresses, sleeping bags, and women while we slept. Can't light the fire 'cos the women up in the tree house would be smoked out . . . ho hum. A lazy day . . . women in the tree house make music, Io's clarinet sticking out through the reeds . . . women sing, juggle, Babs and Alison entertain with fire-eating.

Half the camp go to the pub in the evening . . . about six of us remain with donated wine, cigarettes, chocolate. A decadent evening! Wine, women and song! Beatrice begins to string up webs between gates, over our heads, and we all join in . . . Babs decorates them with flowers . . . it's beautiful. Tonight our beds are raised on pallets!

*21 May, Friday.* Days last forever and merge with each other . . . time stands still. While we are still lying in our sleeping bags, in front of the gate, two MOD police come with knives and cut down the webs that sway above us, and the banners that decorate the gates. Are they afraid of what they don't understand? It's beautiful and they call it garbage. We rescue a web and hang it from the lamp-post . . . they tell us they own the lamp-post as well. Go to the pub in the evening with Katrina, Jane and Beatrice . . . as Beatrice relaxes, smiles and says she feels better than she has for weeks, I find the loud heavy music and crush of men having the opposite effect . . . and wish I was back where the music is our own.

Drifting to sleep under the polythene, listening to the sound of the rain, I hear an American voice loud and clear: 'If it was up to me I'd pour gasoline over them and burn them.'

# 6
# 'I'll Swear on the Goddess'

On Thursday, 27 May 1982, at 10 o'clock in the morning after a very wet night, police and bailiffs arrived at the camp. Eviction!

We were sitting in the blockade across the main gate when several vans turned up full of policemen, 100 in all. The women who had planned to do direct action were away in Newbury doing the washing, so Amanda and Tina climbed into the tree house. There was a very good view from there and they could see more of the base and a large area around the camp.

A bailiff shouted to them from the ground and told them that unless they moved from the tree house he would order it to be pulled down with them inside it. So they stayed up there. Below, policemen lined up, grinning sadistically.

The police procrastinated for about 15 minutes. Then they returned with the warning that the women would be arrested when they came down. The police put a ladder up against the tree, all the while being thoroughly patronising and making sexist comments. The bailiff climbed up the tree and caught hold of Amanda's arm and lowered her to a policeman standing on the ladder. The rest of the women who weren't still on the blockade, were standing underneath, singing as the two women were brought down.

Then the bulldozers moved in. The bailiff's workers got a landrover and attached chains to it and to the structure – the communal shelter. The poplar tree that was in the middle started swaying and almost broke in half, but the main part of the structure didn't move that much at all. Most of the polythene had already been ripped off by then, but the wooden framework stood up to a lot of tugging.

Eventually the structure was demolished and they started clearing up the mess they had made. The tree was very badly damaged, having most of its lower branches and sticks torn off. We were relieved to see they had not pulled out any roots.

The women arrested for resisting eviction were detained at Newbury Police Station overnight and tried the next morning. Here are some records of their trial at Newbury Magistrates' Court on 28 May.

'The court will stand.' Restlessness. Some bob up and grab their seated neighbours' sleeves, yanking them to their feet. The rest of us are real comfortable as we are. We are warned. Disobedience could go against the women on trial here today.

One more chance. 'The court will stand.'

We rose.

We sat.

It begins . . .

'On the 27th May you were a disturbance to a bailiff in the course of his duty to the Queen, and you thoughtfully, wilfully and persistently obstructed . . . under the authority of a High Court Order . . . in removing the camp from outside the RAF base . . . and hereby caused a breach of the peace.'

Two men police officers stand in front of the door. Two women police officers stand guarding the public gallery. Eyes everywhere . . . all over you.

Amanda: 'No.'

Sarah: 'No.'

Beatrice: 'I don't understand, I need a translation . . .'

Io: 'No.'

Tina: 'No.'

The bailiff gives his evidence.

(Humming from the dock.)

The defendants look at one another in total disbelief.

Sarah sits in the dock making webs of wool.

(Humming gets louder and louder as the bailiff continues.)

The solicitor for the defence asks for the list of names on the eviction order, to see if the defendants are on it.

Lady magistrate, poker-faced, doesn't speak and looks worried.

Prosecution: 'Er . . . I would suggest that these are "persons unknown".'

Bailiff: 'I arrived around 10 o'clock and there were a number of young ladies sitting in the entrance to the main gate and another two well, just, well . . . walking around. My colleague approached them and introduced himself . . . said he had a warrant from the Queen's Bench and would they go voluntarily otherwise he would have to carry out the orders of the court. They made comments. "If this is common land," they said, "you have no right to move us" and "If we were having a picnic, would you come and move us off?"

'My colleague said he merely held the warrant and had his orders to carry out. He was giving the ladies these instructions, as he had been told to do.'

(Humming swells.)

Bailiff continues: '. . . It wasn't for us to decide what was what. My colleague reminded the ladies that his job was simply to obey orders.'

Sniggers from the public gallery.

Bailiff again: 'This kind of reaction is quite unusual . . . we move gypsies . . . have dealt with them very satisfactorily . . . we get in sub-contractors to tow vehicles away . . . clear the site . . .

'Whilst we were carrying out our duty, the young ladies followed us around carrying something and singing. At the point when the bulldozer was pulling down the erection, two young ladies started walking around it and tying it up with pieces of string. We approached them and asked them to move out of the way.' (Louder humming.) 'They did move . . . I'm not sure what happened next but suddenly one of the young ladies appeared in the cabin of the Colt. The driver got in the other side and . . . forced her removal. She was sort of "put out". Well, then she came round the front of the bulldozer and two or three others joined her. There was a lot of squealing and hand clapping. We asked them to move . . . [humming fills the courtroom] . . . because they were endangering their lives.

'They ignored us and carried on singing. So we asked the police, who were standing by, to remove them. More ladies went and sat in front of it and we again asked them to move as they were obstructing us in the use of our warrant.

'. . . Then one of the ladies was hit in the shoulder . . .'

Another bailiff: 'The girls still maintained their place at the main gate and then they, of course, had to be removed. I personally warned all the girls that their obstruction was liable to arrest. [Humming reaches high pitch.] I then told them their persistent singing or silence would be taken as a negative response, so after

48

they refused to move, we did bodily remove them.'

Clerk interrupts: 'A woman here on a driving offence has to get home to feed her baby . . .'

Magistrate: 'Can't the baby-sitter feed her baby?'

Clerk disappears.

Defence: 'Did you show a warrant?'

Bailiff shows the court the warrant in his hand.

Defence: 'Can you identify the defendants? I see the order was not attached and, anyway, only one of the defendants is named . . . as a person unknown! I therefore question this court's authority to impose a bind over on these people. If that was to be done, it could apply to anyone, in fact, everyone in this court today.'

Prosecution: 'That order was given to repossess the land. Therefore, anyone found . . . could be the subject of these proceedings . . .'

Magistrate decides to proceed and calls another witness.

Sub-contracted driver: 'They asked me to remove the structure from the site. That's when the girls got in front of the machine. They stood there and a couple walked round with woollen string, going round and round with it. Some more girls came along and laid down in front of it. At one point a girl got in the cab and I had to get back in and get her out, which I did . . .'

Police officer: 'At approximately 12.10 I went to the main gate to get PC . . . and other officers. I saw situated around the main gate a number of caravans and wigwams made of poles . . . and about 15 women. At about 12.30 I saw a caterpillar as it arrived near the wigwams. I saw four or five women run towards it and lie down, in front, to deliberately obstruct its progress. They remained where they were, so I went to the woman I knew to be Beatrice Schmidt and I said, "Do you understand English?" She said, "Yes." I said, "You are being asked to move . . . I'm instructing you to move as you are obstructing the tractor." [Ear-piercing hums.] She made no reply. Together with PC . . . I picked her up and moved her out of the way . . . this was at approximately, er . . . um . . . and then I saw the tractor move off and in no time at all I saw Miss Schmidt run in front of it yet again, and sit down in front of it. I went up to her and said, "You have already been warned . . . [humming from the dock gets louder] . . . about your conduct and I am arresting you for conduct likely to cause a breach of the peace." She again made no effort to reply . . . It is not true that one of the police officers stepped on her bare feet . . . yes, her feet were in the way . . . and I did, yes I did move them back . . .'

Humming much, much louder.

Another police officer is called to the witness stand.

Police officer 2: 'At about 12.15 a bulldozer arrived on a low loader. Four or five women moved directly in front of it. They sat down and didn't move. They held on to each other. I recognised two of them . . . by that time Miss Oliver had arrived and was lying on her back with her head under the bulldozer holding on to the girl next to her. She made no reply when I cautioned her. She did not make any attempt to move. We had to remove her to the side. At approximately 12.45 the driver stopped his machine. Four women stood in front of the loader and linked arms. Miss Oliver was one of them. They were quickly identified and taken away by the officers. Miss Oliver refused to walk to the side, away from the vehicle, and had to be carried. Pardon? Yes . . . I did hear Schmidt screaming . . .'

Defence: 'What was the reason for the screaming?'

Police officer: 'I assume it was because her hand was hurt.'

Police officer 3: 'I saw Miss Green climb into the cab of the bulldozer. She put her arm against the door to stop it being opened. My colleague got in the other side and she was quietly removed and then arrested for causing a breach of the peace. I twice said to her . . . [humming begins again] . . . I twice said to her, "You are advised not to return." We escorted her away and said she was not to go back. She immediately returned to block the gate. We chased her . . .'

'No! . . .,' Sarah yells from the dock.

PC continues: 'That is all the evidence I wish to present.'

The magistrate calls the first witness for the defence.

Helen John: 'We have been living non-violently at the peace camp for eight months. We have never abused or hurt anyone. We have all along acted very peacefully. The way the bailiff's officers were carrying on was very distressing to us as they were causing unnecessary damage and hurting us, too. We built a treehouse without putting a single nail into the live wood. We weren't violent in any way. One of the women simply went into the cab to make the point that they were damaging the tree . . .'

The defendants' turn.

Sarah Green: 'I'll swear on the goddess but not on the god.'

Magistrate: 'You don't wish to take the oath in the accepted form?'

Sarah: 'It is acceptable to me if it is the goddess.'

Magistrate nods.

Sarah: 'The only person who has talked sense today is Helen. The rest of the time we have been dealing with technicalities, not reality. At this moment the Cruise missiles could start off a holocaust. We are all supposed to be reasonable people . . . instead of dealing with technicalities, why can't we sit down together and with our hearts and minds, search for peace?

'I have evidence of one of the police officers treating me violently . . . there is another officer who saw it . . .'

Magistrate: 'Please forgive me if I interrupt, but if this complaint is made here, they won't have a chance to reply. There is a formal complaints procedure . . . Please confine yourself to yesterday.'

Sarah: 'But that's the whole point, no one is dealing with the real problem – violence! We are only here to talk about yesterday! Since then all the officers have got together to match up their statements and fill them with warnings and cautions . . . but there were no cautions yesterday . . . we never heard any warnings . . .'

Beatrice: 'I don't want to swear by a god, only by the life of my children.

'Two policemen took me very roughly and caught me on the pavement. I saw how all the other women who had also laid down under the dulldozer were also carted away. The bulldozer moved then, on to the other side of the tree, and broke a very big living branch down. We went to that living branch to take it away and plant it again when the bulldozer moved again and I was beaten very bad by a piece of wood which moved because of the bulldozer. We then took the branch away and I was standing about 10 metres away from the bulldozer when three women stood in front of it to stop it. I saw how they brought Amanda and Tina away and turned . . . I wanted that they would also bring the other 30 women but suddenly I was knocked down by a big branch. Nobody told me to mind away, and I couldn't know this big branch would come down because the bulldozer was so far away.

'Some women then helped me to get up again. I turned round and three minutes later I saw Sarah stand near the bulldozer. I went to her and in that minute I heard someone say crossly, "We told you we would arrest you" and at the same time they took me so roughly that I am struggling with my arm because I have big bloody holes in it and my hand. They brought me then in the police van and after I moved my right foot two times out of the van again, one policeman holds my foot with his foot back in the van. When he entered the van he jumped wilfully on to my foot so that I couldn't stop screaming . . .

'I am asked to promise that I didn't breach the peace again. I want to say that I never did breach the peace, so I can promise you that I'll always go on and try and keep the peace. I'll always go on for my children . . . and for all those other women's lives . . .'

Tina Oliver: 'The charge brought against me is that of obstructing a bailiff's officer in the execution of his duty. My reason was to prevent the unnecessary damage of a living thing. I don't accept that the unnecessary damage of a living thing was included in the bailiff's duty and therefore do not accept the charge.'

Ioma Ax: 'I would like to make two points. The first, is wrongful arrest. On Monday 24 May I visited Stove Hall in Reading and looked at maps that referred to the Greenham Common area. I spoke to the person in charge there and discovered that the road outside the main gates of USAF base at Greenham does not exist on any maps and does not belong to Newbury District Council . . . or, at least, on Monday it didn't! This is why I took the action I did, because to my understanding, the bailiffs seemed to be unaware of these facts.

'The second point is about the charge of breach of the peace. I have been trying to bring peace about by my intent and actions at Greenham Common to stop Cruise missiles being sited there, and it seems ironical that I am now charged with actions likely to cause breach of the peace!

'I do not accept your laws or your justice while these laws are invented and acted upon by men of violence and some women who also choose to accept these patriarchal laws which will bring genocide even closer and will exterminate your children as well as ours . . . there is no difference.'

Sings

> You can forbid nearly everything
> But you can't forbid me to think
> And you can't forbid my tears to flow
> And you can't shut my mouth when I sing.

Magistrate: 'We ask you to enter into recognisance and to keep the Queen's peace for the next twelve months for the sum of £25.

Are you willing to accept?'

Amanda: 'No.'

Sarah: 'I will follow my own morality. If these people continue to do what they are doing, preparing for nuclear war, then I will continue what I am doing.'

Beatrice: 'Yes, I will keep the peace, as I always have.'

Ioma: 'I do not accept your wording or your values. I believe I have always kept the peace.'

Magistrate: 'Will you answer the question? Yes or no?'

Ioma: 'No.'

Magistrate: 'Is that no . . . which question are you answering?'

Ioma: 'I must follow my own morality.'

Magistrate: 'I think we must take that as "No".' He looks around at the other magistrates on either side of him. They nod their approval of his interpretation.

Tina: 'Yes, I'll keep the peace, but I'll use my own definition of peace.'

Magistrate: 'You must answer "Yes" or "No".'

Tina: 'I shall use my own interpretation.'

Magistrate: 'Then we must ask the court to decide.'

Helen: 'The rules of this court don't seem adequate to deal with this subject matter . . .!'

Jayne: 'You must stop hiding behind that bar and have courage!'

Magistrates mumble.

'Seven days!'

'Shame! Shame!' booms a woman in the gallery. 'A shame on this court!'


*In the next Greenham newsletter Sarah Green wrote an account of what happened to them when they went to prison:* Four women from the peace camp have just spent a week in Holloway for allegedly refusing to be bound over to keep the peace. All of us stated that our lives were dedicated to working towards peace, and we would continue to do this. When we arrived at Holloway we asked for political status on the grounds that the only reason we were there was because our moral and political beliefs differed from those in power who were sending us to prison. We were told that Britain does not recognise political prisoners and that the only people in prison are criminals. This was obviously not correct as we were there at the time. It was a bit of a shock being taken off so suddenly to Holloway, but we made the decision in the van on the way that instead of being apprehensive we would look forward to arriving at Holloway and we should learn as much as possible from our visit.

I certainly learned a lot. Holloway is just the same as any other authoritarian institution. Most of the women were young, in their teens and early twenties, most were black or Irish and a lot of the women were inside for very trivial things: shoplifting, false cheques, soliciting, loitering or non-payment of fines. At the same time as confining these women, society praises and rewards the real criminals: the controllers of money, the arms dealers, the military men who are prepared to kill and the nuclear physicists who invent more efficient ways to destroy the planet each day. To keep a woman in Holloway from one week to the next costs approximately £170.

The second day that we were in prison, we were moved to a short-term convicted prisoners' wing called A4. The women were a little dubious of us at first. Later it turned out they had all been warned not to talk to us, or listen to a word we said. We got on well with the women and most of them were very interested in what we were doing. Like most people, they didn't want more nuclear bombs in this country but didn't feel they could do anything about it, or that they even had a right to.

We were lucky that we arrived on Friday so we had the weekend and Bank Holiday to settle in before we were expected to work. We were taken to a workroom set out with tables, where women were assembling toy space ships called Alien Space Invaders. Women were expected to fit guns on to the machines and put them in boxes, with the firm name 'Britain' on them, covered in union jacks. We sat at our table humming and I informed the man in charge that we did not intend to take part in the work because these were war toys. He said that he had never heard such rubbish and that we would lose all our remission and pay if we did not do this *voluntary* work. Later he came back to the table and insisted on showing us how to assemble the machines. We started singing, 'Take the toys away from the boys'. The man was extremely disturbed and shouted to the women guards, 'Get them out of here!' Most of the women were very amused by this. We were not asked to work again.

While I was in there I felt very confident that I could survive, but when I was released I was filled with such sadness to know that all those women were still there and that I had to live in a society that so happily accepts and works for this. This is the same society that

54

builds the weapons to destroy the world because it thinks it can do no different.

I hasten to disagree. We want a different society – society is only people and people can change things.

# 7
# Dying to Live

During the June 1982 CND demonstration in London, a woman from Greenham spoke at the Hyde Park rally. She asked any women wanting to take action the next day, to coincide with President Reagan's arrival in London, to meet over by the trees. A crowd gathered. *Among them was Gillian Booth:*

We are beginning to make our plans to go down to Greenham Common again, but first there's Reagan, our Ronnie, due to arrive in London and we can't let his visit pass without comment.

And how best to greet this gentleman (sic) when at the invitation of Margaret Thatcher and our own unpleasant government, he arrives here in London, favourite city of the Americans but of few English?

The answer to this duly arrived as we were sitting on the grass at this large gathering of concerned souls in Hyde Park, a little breeze passed us inviting us to die. Or pretend to.

It seemed that some women had something up their sleeves and had organised a direct action which required bodies to block traffic at various strategic points in the centre of London; a die-in no less, England having gotten Americanised in the 12 years I was away. Lie in the road and pretend to be dead while some women hand out leaflets explaining what a rotten deal Thatcher, Reagan et al are handing us in terms of expectation of survival and while these same women hopefully protect those of us who decide to 'die' from any inappropriate, untoward response on the part of the general public. Or perhaps the police. Then a leaflet came round telling us how to die and whom to contact in the event of one's demise. And at the end of it all, innocently added on, was a request for assembly in Jubilee Gardens on the following day at 7 a.m.

? . . . Did they say *seven*?

Yup, they said seven. We actually did get down to Jubilee Gardens by 7 a.m. and I had fried egg and potatoes and toast too because I couldn't die on an empty stomach. And all those poor women made it by 7 a.m. too. And I didn't feel too scared at the thought of lying down on a city of London street in the middle of rush hour because it sunk in the day before that I was actually going to do that when we were all sitting under the trees in Hyde Park near the terrible photographs of that 16-year-old girl that the Iranians were showing, all you could see were her eyes, the photograph was taken after all the torture they did to her before they shot her by firing squad, 16, and who took the photograph? I started to freak out because I got scared right then and Arlene said what if a car runs over you and I got scared thinking of that and police and torture and out it all came blah-ah-ah and it was like that story when he says has anyone got any valium and absolutely everyone has some except that all these little phials of Bach flower rescue remedy were popping up around me.

We know this much, that the die-in which our particular group is doing will not be on the main drag, as some groups will be, but down a side street that motorists might use as an escape route. We come up the street, our leader rushes ahead. Arlene looks pale, my stomach kills, knees feel woolly, the flower remedy phials are passing round like crazy now. As we cross a street, suddenly we are engulfed by a huge grey wave of office workers, military provision of skirts and tailored trousers, and ah, those many pointed umbrellas. Dear god it was all this time a tyre crushing in my head I was fearing, not to be confronted by irate pedestrians with pointed missiles. For one moment I fear I shall throw up then the moment is over and I'm with a group of women striding through the early morning heat to a destination only one of us knows, getting looked at by 100 passers-by who could be inhabitants of another planet they seem that different but who I know will burn and shrivel up the same as me if the bomb fell in the clear light on such a Monday morning.

I used to burn flies' wings.

Our leader says OK you can do it, five of us lie down and five of us stay up, our leader stays up, Arlene stays up. I walk to the centre of the road, I see nothing but Arlene as I lie down. I go first on my side then I roll over, another woman comes and lies down next to me, she lies with her face up, she does not look much older than 16. I cup my hand against my face so that my cheek will be protected from the hard surface of the road, I lie there smelling the faint odour of sewage coming from somewhere, the voices rise and swell around me, the traffic revs and roars, I give myself up, my eyes are one inch from the ground, I think of the eyes of the girl they tortured in Iran the month we left America to come to England, the 16-year-old baby girl in Iran what did they do to you darling what did they do to you . . .

The camp was now very definitely a women's place. We were learning the joys of being woman-identified – being able to be and do, without having to please men in anyway. But we still have tow ork through old, established patterns of dominance and submission.

*Babs Schmidt is a German woman, who was studying drama at a college in England. She came to the March blockade and then moved to the camp:* It was a hot summer that August 1982. We still lived in caravans then and the place had something of a holiday camp atmosphere. The group was small and there was much space for new thoughts and old fears to be shared. Yet it was going to be the most difficult time I ever spent at the camp.

Anger flared up – misunderstandings, confrontations. Womyn being called violent, womyn getting frightened, feeling hurt. I couldn't switch off. I couldn't find a distance to anything. Everything was directly attached to being a womun, to growing as womyn.

But there was also the aim – the one big blob we tried so desperately to define. Why are we here? How do we want things to change and how are we going to change them? Big words floating about. Non-violence, middle-class mentality, leadership – big words, big judgements. Everything was big except our patience for each other. What a dilemma. We had to be impatient with patriarchy, with their bombs, and at the same time we had to be extremely patient with each other.

If it hadn't been for those magic moments when we were full of dreams and weird ideas, it would have seemed to me that that would have been the end of a wonderful attempt to save the world.

Next thing was Hiroshima Day, 6 August.

'How many died?'

'One hundred thousand in the first instant!'

Graves, gravestones, stones. We set out to collect one hundred thousand stones to be placed on the Newbury War Memorial during a whole day's mourning and vigil.

I will never forget the first hundred stones. The shape, the texture, the coldness of the stones and the endless images! Yes, this

58

was real. I did know why I was here. I think we all did. It was so damn real, it turned my guts upside down. We were obsessed with getting the one hundred thousand stones together and time was running out . . . twenty-four hours left, sixteen hours, two hours, half an hour, ten minutes. The last stone. Quick! All in the cars.

What has that to do with the bomb? Well, picking up those stones and putting them on the concrete steps which said 'For the Glory of the Dead' made more sense to me than most things I've done in my life.

Newbury was hostile but 80 people put down a stone themselves. 'This is one person's life. Do you want to honour it by placing this stone with the others?' I heard myself saying a hundred times an hour. An old man, a war veteran, slapped me in the face.

'Where would we be if we hadn't fought the Japs?'

Womyn screaming at us, 'My husband died for the likes of you!' The national front lined up. The police offered to arrest us to keep the public peace. They made it sound as if they were doing us a favour. We didn't want to get arrested that day. Two days later, August 9, was Nagasaki Day and we had plans to go inside the base. We didn't want to leave the stones, either. We tried to make a deal with the Council that they would deliver the stones to the camp so we could build a peace cairn with them. They agreed. We left. They did nothing. Instead, Newbury womyn arrived with shopping bags and carried the stones away. Imagine, shopping bags and all. At least they touched the stones, I told myself, but the knot in my stomach tightened up another inch or two.

We all reacted differently to the hostility in Newbury and once back at the camp, the whole discussion about non-violence flared up again. It was as if we were judging each other, giving marks for good or bad behaviour. Well, it is difficult. If you care a lot for an action then you prepare yourself for it. You imagine how you'd like it to be and if another womun goes against your sensitivity, it causes gut reactions.

We hadn't yet learned to communicate all this beforehand, so we had to do it afterwards and it proved to be a very destructive, painful exercise. Non-violence doesn't stand up in theory unless you are able to live it. And then where does it start, where does it end?

There was very little time to work through things because the next day we were out for the biggy. None of us had set foot in the base up till then and we were all geared up to meet men with dogs and guns and prison sentences up to fourteen years. At night, I think, everyone felt pretty scared and alone. It was like writing your last will, saying good-bye to all sorts of people and pleasures.

The intensity of the day before the action was hardly bearable. There we were, hunched up in a caravan, looking for bugs and spies, trying to be honest with each other. We all weren't so sure any more if we trusted each other enough to go in there as one. It was difficult saying to a womun that you didn't feel good about her taking part in the action and why. But it felt very necessary. I mean, can you imagine letting yourself into something like that without trusting each other? You might end up in a cell with someone you really can't cope with. We were all forced into a closeness that felt difficult to comprehend. And we also needed to make the action as safe as possible. Only if we were calm did we stand a chance of coming out of it all right. No aggression or tension inside.

Most of our meetings took place in secrecy because we were afraid that if they found out about it beforehand they would do us for conspiracy. I am sure lots of womyn felt excluded and hurt by that. In the end eight of us formed a group and we knew we were going in.

A Japanese womun had sent us a letter with a very touching story in it about a young girl who got injured by the Nagasaki bomb, and suffered great pain in hospital. She believed that if she could fold a thousand paper cranes, there would never be another war. She finished nine hundred and ninety-nine and then died. Ever since, the paper crane has been a peace symbol in Japan.

We decided to make the thousandth paper crane and to deliver it to the Commander of the base with the request that he hand it to Reagan. We all dressed in black and white with paper lotuses all over us and flowers and other nice things that we wanted to take inside. We chose the New Age Gate (now Blue Gate) and just walked slowly and confidently past the guard who was hobbling alongside us, waving his arms, ordering us to stop. The camera crew was staged outside the gates so we stayed in view, sat down in a circle holding hands and were joined by a whole group of spiders of all sizes and colours.

It was very peaceful sitting there in the sun. There was no traffic, no noise except the by now totally confused MOD man talking over his CB. After half an hour (!) we were politely asked to leave. We replied with a request to see the Commander. He arrived with a crew of men in uniform, took the letter and the paper crane and ordered the men to put us into a van. We wouldn't move so they

60

picked us up and the big boss was ever so worried about our welfare. 'Gently, gently, don't bump their heads' he would repeat over and over again. They gave us a sight-seeing tour round the base that proved very useful in later actions, and then chucked us out at the Forgotten Gate (now Violet Gate) where, by sheer coincidence, the American chief of the base took a last look at us (hanging in the arms of the MOD) and said, 'Gee, that is going too far.' It wasn't, I tell you. We've only just started.

After recovering from the shock of not being interrogated by the CID, not being tortured or imprisoned for life, we knew we wanted to go in more often. We had the reassurance of acting together, but the criticism of the womyn who didn't take part for various reasons, now had to be listened to. The wound was still open, anger and pain were still there and we spent long hours shouting, crying and talking to each other. My initial shock at how much we all have to learn in order to respect, tolerate, care and love each other and nature, was unresolved and at the end of that summer I fled back to London and caught up with the 'down to earth' life among Bermondsey womyn. It took me six months of retreat to understand I'd been observing the symptoms of patriarchy, not patriarchy itself, while watching myself and others coping with womun power in a different, rather than oppressive way.

*Before Babs left, an exciting new dream began to take shape; a dream that was to bring women together in a big way:* I remember the morning in the kitchen caravan, where we all asked each other what we would like to do most. 'Surround the base! . . . link arms!'

Nobody said, 'That's impossible'. Immediately all of us raided our heads for the last leftovers from maths lessons, and we worked out we needed ten thousand womyn, at least. Sixteen thousand to make sure. And we all agreed that we wouldn't tell the press any numbers so if fewer womyn turned up, it would still be a success.

Well, I've never seen anything like it. Two weeks later we started with the leaflets. We needed this focus to experience our strength as a group.

# 8
# We Are Here to Stay

A few weeks after the eviction in May, the Ministry of Transport (MOT) secured a High Court Order for our removal from their land, and ever since they had been declaring their intention to put this into effect. In the midst of our expectations of an imminent eviction, the Welsh women arrived . . . They had been scheming.

That evening everyone crammed into the creche caravan in case there were directional microphones set up in the base that could pick up the discussion. The Welsh women revealed their plans. They wanted to go into the base through the main gate and occupy the MOD sentry box.

With the eviction hanging over our heads, all the attention was on our so-called trespass, but that was not the issue at all. It was not between us and the MOT, whose land we were camped on, it was between us and the MOD. The issue was Cruise missiles. By going into the base we could bring the focus back to the trespass of US bases on our homeland.

*Rebecca Johnson had arrived at Greenham three weeks earlier, having decided to postpone her postgraduate studies for what she considered more important work at the camp. She was at that meeting:* One of the Welsh women spoke and she put it so compellingly, the urgency, the imminence of what was happening, the way in which they'd already started stepping up the big lorries going into the base at night, the building programme and cutting down the trees all around the edges of the base. I thought, 'No, I can't be anxious about an MA thesis. I can't be an academic ostrich. I've actually got to do something.' First I found myself deciding to take action and then suddenly I was being handed a press release to put together.

The next morning we woke early to a glorious sunny day. Zero hour was 10 a.m. and we were all on tenterhooks. Reporters were supposed to be coming but at that time it was very hard to persuade the press to turn up because as far as they were concerned, we were just a bunch of women sitting outside a base – so what!

For what seemed like hours we hung around the kitchen caravan having long, drawn-out cups of tea and coffee, convinced that we looked really suspicious. Then at 10 o'clock we started walking casually up towards the main gate. As we got closer, the sentry box guard came rushing out, his arms flapping about, and headed straight for Helen, 'Now, now, ladies, you're not allowed in here.'

Helen kept walking straight towards him and I just thought, 'The sentry box is open – go for it!'

The guard immediately made a grab for Helen while everyone else rushed into the box and shut the door. Some weren't quick enough and were shut out so they sat on the ground outside singing and whooping. Helen, crippled with laughter, was led out while being asked, 'What's going on Mrs John? You're not silly enough to be involved in this are you?'

No sooner was she put out, than she ripped back in when he wasn't looking!

*Rebecca*: It was amazing – my heart was really thumping and I was feeling very slightly sick but quite excited. By now the guard was knocking on the windows, looking very upset and angry. 'What's the matter?' we asked. It finally emerged that his breakfast and his spectacles were inside. We opened a little side window and handed them out to a woman on the outside who gave them to him. He was kind of nonplussed that we'd done this for him – he'd worked himself up into quite a bad temper – and when we handed his things out he didn't know what to do.

Inside the sentry box the telephone rings.

'Women's Peace Camp,' says a cheerful voice on the phone.

No answer. The fourth time the phone rings there is a response from the other end.

'Gee, I didn't know you all had a phone down there now.'

'Yes,' comes the reply, 'it's yours.'

The police are still trying to release a jammed gate with a sledgehammer so that they can lock it, but are hampered by women singing and dancing and weaving webs of wool between the wire-mesh.

Twenty minutes later an open cattle-type truck drives up and parks between the sentry box and the gate to try and break visual contact between us. The singing gets louder and some women climb the gate posts to keep the others in view.

*Rebecca*: Then two van loads of police arrived. They jumped out and rushed at the sentry box. We'd opened a couple of the small windows because some women were smoking and it was also very hot. The first thing I realised was a policeman's arm coming through a small window. My instinctive reaction was to slam the window shut to immobilise him, but I realised if I did that I would hurt him. So we had to watch as his arm reached in and got the catch of a larger window open, and then they were in.

We'd achieved our purpose now and we went limp, but kept on singing as they carried us out, one by one. Chris, one of the Welsh women, was wearing a large badge saying, 'I'm pregnant – please handle with care' and they weren't sure how to handle her so they left her till last. They were quite gentle with us then – but that was in the early days – they just lifted us into the police van and took us to the police station. We did a lot of singing and talking to the policemen and women and it felt really good.

After we got out we had a meeting and decided to look for feminist lawyers who would understand what we'd done, who would argue the case politically and would let us speak for ourselves.

We were successful in that search and the lawyers we found, Jane Hickman, Isabel Forshall and Elizabeth Woodcraft, became an integral part of our campaign.

It is now September and still the eviction hasn't happened. The threat, and how we will survive afterwards, occupies our thoughts. *Jane Lockwood, who'd recently left art college, had been living at the camp for several months. She kept a diary which reflects much of what happened and how many of us felt:*

*14 September* – I have some good news. Sarah is going to have a baby! She's so happy, everyone is. She's been trying for so long. It's one of the nicest pieces of news we've had. Also Sarah and Jayne have come up with more ideas to get the action on 12 December moving.

There's more helicopter activity tonight. Over the past few weeks helicopters have been flying in apparently delivering something. I don't like it. Something feels funny about it all. At least four large transporters have gone in tonight coming from Aldermaston direction. We've got no car so we're not able to see if they are delivering something tonight. On Saturday we watched at least three helicopters landing, staying on the ground for no more than two minutes then taking off and reappearing ten minutes later to drop something else. There was a lot of activity on the runway; lorries and cars going up and down, some going towards the silo area . . . it could be some sort of practice.

Some women came back from Newbury with gossip about what people in Newbury are saying and some news about the Council. The Council are putting the local rates up– and the news is that local people say it's because of the extra police work because of us that they have to pay higher rates. That'll do us the world of good locally – it's disgraceful the way the authorities work, trying to get the locals to hate us enough to attack us. Sooner or later someone at the camp is going to be very badly hurt or even raped – it's a miracle things haven't been worse up to now. Apparently the Council made a statement on TV that they are going to sue us for £20,000 for the costs of our eviction. They've not approached us as they are certainly on to a loser.

*15 September* – Cold damp evening, but very clear after a really hot day. Things have been very mellow today, quiet and calm. We have decided to send letters out to the women on the register from the 21 March action, a sort of chain letter that they can send on to more women. We'd really like thousands of women to come and hold hands around the base, singing, dancing, chanting around the perimeter fence. We've got a list of maybe 300 women, so 1,000 women for 12 December after all the publicity for it in peace magazines and women's magazines isn't a far off dream really. Barbara is going to photocopy them so we can mail them to women all over England in the next few days.

The kids are very interested in Sarah's baby in her belly. They've been asking so many questions – it's really beautiful.

The day-to-day running of the camp and preparations for 12 December were taking most of our time, but we still had to reserve some energy for the sentry box trial due on 20 September.

*Rebecca*: We were totally unprepared for the court case. I had packed a bag to go to prison but I was terrified because of what that would mean.

We went along hoping for an adjournment and to everyone's immense surprise it was granted until November so that we could get legal aid and call witnesses. That just knocked us flat. It gave us two months.

Finally, on 29 September, the bailiffs arrived to evict the camp. *Charlie Kiss had just left school and after visiting Greenham with her mother she had moved here with her mother's full support. She was now attending the local college. She remembers a rude awakening:* For the past months I'd been studying for my 'A' levels at Newbury, which meant getting up early and cycling on the camp bike to college. That morning I woke up, pulled back the caravan curtains, only to see that it was raining hard. It was only 9 o'clock so I went back to sleep again, thankful I didn't have to leave until ten. The next time I woke up I glanced out the window to see police vans and lots of police up by the fence. Straight away I knew it was the eviction. Mandy, who was also in the caravan, came over to the window. At first we were a bit stunned. Then we thought that other women must still be asleep or reading and would have no idea we were about to be evicted. So we rushed around waking and telling the women, 'The eviction's finally come'.

*Mary Millington found herself in the middle of the chaos:* Soon everyone was packing up tents and bedding and hiding them, looking for places to put things we would need for the next stage of the camp's life. Saucepans, food, cutlery, cash and bedding were packed into cars; we hid our standpipe very carefully. Meanwhile it rained solidly. Some women went to Angela's to ring the press. Others took car loads of belongings to Barbara's house to store. More than thirty policemen stood around as the cranes lifted our caravans on to the transporters.

There were 11 of us there that day but we didn't feel outnumbered. Some of us spoke to the press who took photographs, then we all linked arms and sang, 'You can't kill the spirit, she is like a mountain, old and strong she goes on and on . . .' We sang for hours, feeling calm and happy, standing, swaying in a line faced by an embarrassed line of policemen. Two local women who came to support, joined the singing and were soon in tears.

Once the caravans were removed, bulldozers scraped away the

remaining signs of our occupation; a bailiff's worker struggled with one of Jayne's red wool webs, hacking at it with an axe.

A TV crew arrived and graciously provided a white umbrella as a neutral backdrop in the pouring rain while they interviewed women. When the interview was over, Jayne half-jokingly suggested that they might like to donate the umbrella. The answer was an embarrassed 'No'.

*Mary*: Meanwhile women sat themselves down on the bench by the bus stop and began to plan our survival for the night, and watched as the first lorry load of stones and rocks from Somerset were dumped on what had been our home. Two of us went to gather heather to make a mattress, while other women arrived and reacted to the scene of destruction, some with tears.

After the first shock of seeing these great boulders dumped – it was going to be landscaped, the workmen told us – we decided to do some landscaping ourselves. Climbing up on to the rocks we joked that they were bringing the mountain to us and sang, 'I have dreamed on this mountain since first I was my mother's daughter and you just can't take my dreams away.'

Mandy had rescued a plastic bowl, a soggy teabag and a washing brush, and she was elaborately pretending to do the dishes. We carried some rocks over to the fence near the main gate, where the camp had originally been set up, and set about building a fire. Jayne pulled a ball of red wool out of her bottomless bag and began weaving angry red webs across the gorse bushes.

As evening drew in the strain began to show. The devastation of what had been our home, the reality of our plight, to survive on this bleak rock-strewn plot of land on the edge of a highway, the rain falling incessantly in weighted drops, large puddles bursting into a continuous stream – everywhere mud! We were soaked to the skin and although our spirits, together, had carried us through, the cold and damp seeped into our bones.

We went in groups over to Barbara's house to dry out and catch the evening news. It was a bit like walking into the camp indoors. Piles of soggy blankets, sleeping bags, rucksacks, cooking pots, mud and women everywhere.

Later that evening everyone returned to the camp and despite the day's ordeal we had a celebration.

*Jane's diary: 30 September* – Last night was amazing. We moved back on to the old patch, built a fire and a lovely structure which had to be taken down this morning. The police had a go at us at tea-time because of the fire but they seemed to be a bit overpowered by our high spirits.

We slept in our hidden bender last night – it was quite warm and cosy although the condensation is a bit of a problem. This bender is so beautiful – the moon shines in at night, the sun shines through in the daytime, but it's just so peaceful.

Today we got up to a bit of bother to put it lightly. We've been painting the rocks with beautiful things; we've made signs and written words with them but it has to be seen to be believed.

We've had quite a lot of visitors. Helen is up to her usual mischief at the Labour conference – apparently they had a special meeting about us this morning and are doing a special collection. Also even Radio One had an appeal for us today. Things are moving . . .

At least we have plenty of light here. The security lights from the base light up this whole area. I'm so pleased to be back here on this patch, the fire in the same place, no caravans, no tents. It's like it was when the camp first started. Nothing except a fire, blankets, plastic, a bit of food and spirit, determination, joy – yes joy – we feel great. We know they're not going to get rid of us. Now the penny has really dropped – we are not going to go!

# 9
# Wet Weather and War

We had been left with absolutely nothing and the rain just never seemed to stop. In the bushes we had built a few benders (structures of bent branches covered with plastic and anchored in the ground) but for most of us there was no shelter at all. We slept in survival bags on beds of soft, soggy heather. We had umbrellas to put over the children but the police would not allow us to fix them into the ground. Even the portaloos had been taken. We questioned their removal at the time but were told they had to go in case anyone tried camping in them. When any of us disappeared to the bushes, police followed and watched. In fact, we were followed and watched the whole time. Then we found ways round it. We decoyed in and out of the bushes with tents, pretending to look for somewhere to put them up so that those who really were putting them up could get on unhindered. Women were following police following women following police following women. The police soon got tired. Within three days they had given up their little game.

*Jane's diary: 1 October* – The support is just starting to come. Today we got incredible stuff: food, clothes, candles, over £100 in donations, boots, polythene, even disposable knickers. The people coming are all saying, 'We just managed to get this together last night. What do you need? What messages can we pass on? Keep up your spirits, this is only the beginning.'

I rang up the pound today about the caravans that have been evicted to ask if we could collect some of our belongings from them. The man I spoke to wanted to know my name but I didn't want to tell him because I thought if he knew it he might try to sue me for the eviction costs. So, off the top of my head I pronounced myself 'Bridget Evans' and arranged to meet him on Monday.

*2 October* – Aggie and Katrina rang the pound to get their stuff back. Aggie only went and said that she is Bridget Evans as well. So now we both have to go on Monday saying we're Bridget Evans.

[That was just the beginning for Bridget Evans. She became the camp pseudonym for all sorts of occasions, like letters to councillors, to the papers and at times she was our spokesperson to the police and the press.]

*5 October* – It's raining again. Today was eventful, but I'm unable to say how I feel about it all – I'm getting swamped by my emotions, so much is happening . . . the eviction a few days ago, police hassling us and now the sewage pipes and more arrests. We had a bit of a do-da yesterday about it when the workmen turned up to lay the pipes. Back in December 1981 workmen arrived at the camp to lay pipes right through the middle of the camp into the base in preparation for the extra 1,200 American servicemen who are to guard the missiles. We stopped work then by lying in front of the bulldozers and they must have decided to wait until they'd got rid of us. So yesterday we delayed them as much as possible, by jumping in the ditches and lying in front of bulldozers. We put stuff out in the press urgently to try and get women down here today; the telephone tree was activated; we didn't actually stop them but we made things very difficult. We also contacted the union who deal with men being required to wear correct protective clothing.

Well first of all we occupied the site where they wanted to begin digging. For an hour about 20 of us wove a huge web of wool and string across the whole area. We entangled ourselves in it, some women sat amongst the threads, others lay beneath it. We were addressed, in turn, by policemen who told us that we were obstructing the contractors going about their lawful employment and therefore our behaviour was likely to cause a breach of the peace. Then they began to drag us off very roughly, ripping and untangling themselves from the web.

While I was being dragged off, the policeman who had a hold of my arm was twisting it and I thought that if they carried me much further (I was completely limp so all my body weight was on it) my shoulder would be dislocated. I shouted out that they were breaking my arm and they put me down. One policeman leant over me and hissed close to my face, 'You've got the right to walk you know.' We had a brief dialogue where I reminded them that they were being closely watched and also that they are trained to lift someone without hurting them. We were all cautioned then and warned that if we returned we would be arrested.

For a while we joked and laughed and sang songs until some of the workmen appeared and began hammering wooden posts into the ground to line up the trench. Action again! A group of women ran back on to the site and removed the posts and some other equipment including a hammer which was lobbed into the bushes. The police had been amused by our performance until the hammer disappeared, but then they reacted. Unfortunately Rebecca was the most prominent figure standing on a rock in the middle of the group singing. An officer pointed at her and ordered his men to arrest her – they claimed she had thrown the hammer. She was heavily dragged for about 300 yards to a police van inside the main gate of the base. She was amazing. Only a few minutes earlier she'd said to me, 'I think I'll leave quite soon, I don't feel too well and I don't want to get arrested.' But when this happened she was singing loud and strong and she never stopped even though they were hurting her.

The JCB digger then tried to drive out of the base on to the site. So we started again, taking turns in ones or twos we jumped in front of the digger, lay down and were dragged away by the police. It is an unnerving feeling to be lying in front of a machine when you can't see the face of the driver who keeps edging nearer and nearer to you. The great metal shovel spikes on it inches from your body – and he keeps coming, an inch at a time, forward, forward. I don't know how we manage to stay calm at times like this. Even more moving is the support and attitudes of friends watching. They must stand clear and watch this happen. The authorities can lock us up, they can stop us seeing each other, but they can never stop our feeling and support for each other.

But for Rebecca, who'd had no intention of getting arrested and hadn't prepared herself for the possibility, it was a very unhappy experience.

*Rebecca*: It was pouring with rain, I had a terrible cold and an appalling period and suddenly there I was locked away in this little van on the inside of the base, hardly able to see what was going on outside. I cried for a bit, feeling very sorry for myself. Then I saw an American officer go over to the knot of policemen so I stuck my face to the little window and sang as loudly as I could. They moved away. Then a policewoman came and locked the window shut. Every so often a woman would come to the fence and call to me, but too far away to hear. For about an hour I was on my own and then 12 more women got arrested, which was a relief.

At the police station things got worse. I had asked the police for a tampon as soon as I was arrested. At first the police promised to get some, but hours passed. I had begun leaking blood. I was wet through and shivering. I kept on asking and the police changed from promises to obscene jokes about 'Why don't you try a cork?' Finally I was taken to see a doctor who prescribed penicillin because I was in such a bad way. Not very useful. I wanted to refuse to take it but didn't feel strong enough even for that. I just wanted to get out. I was due in London that evening as a friend had got tickets for a concert for my birthday. The police got through to me with their jeers and taunts far more that day than at any other time. How easy for them to humiliate women, to try and break us.

After being charged, everyone was released in the late afternoon. In the following days the media descended on the camp again. Recent and forthcoming events had once more made us news-worthy.

*Mandy's diary: 8 October* – Am total zombie. Spent the night trying to sleep on the floor of the donated 'peace van' . . . wonder how long I can keep going like this. Camp seems to be full of video people . . . interview with Sarah in progress, Skeeter seems to be handling packs of reporters in her own inimitable style. I manage to sit on a stool that collapses into the mud. This is not going to be a good day.

The men from the DHSS arrive at last. They ask us if we're really available for work. Katrina launches into a wonderful speech of how she'd love to do community work and wouldn't it be great to be able to work among the people of Newbury! We all nod enthusiastically and wave a £450 car repair bill at them to show how our donations are eaten up, leaving no money for luxuries such as food, clothing and bus fares! They seem sympathetic – if we can produce records to show that we do not actually live off donations they'll consider raising our dole from £7.70 to the full £18 . . . wow!

Two women arrive from Hull to stay the weekend with sacks of clothes and goodies. The post arrives with a £100 cheque. Maybe today is going to be okay after all!

Sometimes, simply coping with everyday survival, especially in wet weather, takes all our time. Women outside the camp face this constantly too. The immediate day-to-day struggle to keep going leaves little time or energy for anything else. Political issues look so far away.

While we had been preoccupied by too much mud and not enough money, a war was raging in the Atlantic. On 12 January 1982 British agents in Argentina advised the Foreign Office that Argentina had decided to invade the Falkland Islands. In February the SAS were informed they would be going there. On 31 March Argentina invaded and three days later, 3 April, the British task force set sail for the South Atlantic, armed with nuclear weapons. By taking these weapons Britain was already infringing the Treaty of Tlatelolco to which we are signatories and which forbids the proliferation of nuclear weapons in the South Atlantic.

*Babs*: Not quite understanding the political/economic background of this war, which was called a crisis, seeing only what was presented to us through the media, the shock was immense. Daily we were fed with the spectacle of torpedoed warships sinking, men dying and crowds cheering while young men were herded up for cannon fodder. Memories of the first media-documented war, Vietnam, arose. Were they going to use nuclear weapons? Our being at the camp gained urgency while we were desperately waiting for opposition to the Falklands war to grow. Wearing our camp badges meant aligning ourselves with the enemy. Women accused us of backstabbing their sons, husbands and brothers. The censorship in the media tightened, our attempts to draw a link between the missile bases and the Falklands, silenced. Even supporters would talk to us about the dictatorship in Argentina and our so-called democracy. Our country was at war, but we condemn all countries that decide to wage war and because it was ours we would not shut up.

I went on the 'End the Falklands War' march, organised by CND. I got my T-shirt ripped by a young woman, encouraging her children to do the same because I wanted to see their Daddy killed. I felt numbed. I've never lived through a war, yet I have always lived in a war zone, being a woman, wanting to live. We have to change so much in such a short time; will we be ready for it, when we can't stop women cheering their own sons to death?

73

As the war came to an end, some of the facts began filtering out. We learned that Britain had consistently avoided any real attempt at negotiations with Argentina for many years. We learned that the government had been aware of Argentina's intentions for some time. We learned that our prime minister enjoyed warmongering: 'When you've spent half your political life dealing with humdrum issues like the environment . . . it's exciting to have a real crisis on your hands.' (Margaret Thatcher on 14 May 1982.)

We learned that it was good politics to distract the electorate's attention from domestic problems and give a boost to patriotism just before the election. We learned that these political gains and the loss of 255 British lives as well as 800 Argentinians, were more important to the Government than a compromise suggested by the Peruvian peace plan – a plan which was endorsed by the United Nations and was acceptable to Argentina.

We learned that Britain had been supplying the Argentine junta with weapons and expertise right up until April 1982 – weapons the junta used to repress its people and eventually used against Britain. We also learned that a small group of high-ranking British businessmen were exploiting the Falkland Islands through industrial and land ownership while neglecting the islanders' needs. It was the Argentine air services, hospitals and colleges that offered the islanders practical help.

On 12 October 1982 after Argentina had surrendered, the Falklands Victory Parade took place in London. *Lynne Jones, a doctor who had been involved with the camp since early 1982, went with other women to do a symbolic action at the parade. She wrote this letter afterwards (as a pamphlet) to a woman she met there:*

I don't know your name, in spite of having stood beside you all morning on the parade. I never discovered it. But your face stays clearly in my mind – uncomprehending, distressed. It won't go away. That's why I wanted to write – to try and explain.

We'd known about the parade for weeks; known that while ostensibly it was saying 'welcome home' to the soldiers, it would also be saying 'war is glorious' and while saying 'well done boys', it was also praising Mrs Thatcher for sending them to war. We knew that while the hardware, the guns, the tanks, the marching bands would be there for all to see, there would be no coffins. No victims of burns, no drowned sailors. So we had to go ourselves – to say there's nothing glorious about war, and nothing well done about problems solved by killing people. (That's if you can call the problem of the Falklands solved in any way; I still feel sorry for those people living in what has basically become a military garrison.)

We're just a small group of women. We knew it wouldn't be easy to make our point clearly and without offence. For you have to believe from the start we didn't want to offend anyone. It is war and those who cause it that offend us. So we thought we would do it very simply. Go as a group, and in silence turn our backs on the parade. Holding up a banner saying 'Women Turn Their Backs on War'. That was all. We knew that people around us would be hostile, that they would shout and perhaps physically abuse us. Such occasions seem to breed a violence of their own – where no point of view but that of the mob, even one peacefully expressed, can be tolerated. Odd, isn't it? Because the Falklands victory was surely, if nothing else, victory for our 'democratic liberties' including that of freedom of speech – something sadly missing in Argentina.

Well, we prepared ourselves. Some of us took the parts of hostile onlookers so that the others could experience what it would feel like. We organised ourselves so that some would form a cordon of peacekeepers round the actual demonstrators, giving them at least some protection. I was one of these – my job to talk and pacify if possible.

We hadn't prepared ourselves for you however. A plump, smiling woman, your hair freshly done, bright blue eyes, who came and stood right in the middle of our group. You chose us deliberately, you told me, because we weren't too tall and you thought you could get a good view over our shoulders.

It had been a difficult morning before you arrived. We had got there early to get a good place by the barrier. The women holding the banner however had got the sections muddled and had to go up and down to the underground station to get it sorted out. The coming and going alerted the police who got suspicious and searched us. They didn't find the banner (we wore it under our clothes) but they found a leaflet in my bag with the giveaway words 'Feminism and Disarmament' (are they really so frightening?). Anyway they warned us they'd keep their eye on us. Any barracking the troops or jumping the barriers and they'd be down on us like a ton of bricks. Of course we could promise them there would be neither.

It began to get crowded. And you arrived. Friendly from the start, you told me you were worried your camera wouldn't work –

you didn't know how to use it, did I? Or perhaps one of us could take the pictures from the front. Your son would be marching by and you didn't want to miss him. That was when it hit me. How really difficult, almost impossible it was, what we were trying to do. Here you were, in your best clothes, come a long way with your husband to see your son, who'd got home safe from the war, have his moment of glory. Little enough reward for having put up with the horrors of the South Atlantic. And here was I, equally glad your son was safe, and wanting to deprive him of that moment – seeing in it the seed of other wars, from which he might not come back. How could I explain that to you, standing there so pleased and so proud, how could I explain that I thought we had to stop being pleased and proud and be bitter and sad and angry and say, 'It has to stop. There must be another way, some method of solving conflicts that doesn't waste and destroy. Finding it would really give us reason for pride.' I had two hours before the parade came by. If I had tried, would you have listened? Or would you have called the police and had us removed? I don't know because I'm afraid I lacked the courage. I said nothing, but I couldn't bear the thought of how you would feel when we turned around and held up our banner. I didn't want you to miss your son. I asked the woman at the front to find a place for you. You wouldn't take it at first, insisting we were 'too kind', but you gave in and moved next to Karen. I felt like Judas.

The waiting was awful. I saw you chatting and making friends with Karen, everyone does. Your place beside me had been taken by a severe-looking woman in a smart blue hat who eyed me suspiciously and made no attempt to talk. Mary, next to me, was having problems with her child. The man behind her didn't like her baby carrier. But his wife told him to shut up, and told us not to mind – she had grandchildren herself. The child went to sleep. It started to rain. A band somewhere was playing 'hits' from 'The Sound of Music' and 'My Fair Lady' . . . we sang along in a desultory sort of way.

Then the helicopters came. Did you see them? What did you feel? I can only tell you that to me there is nothing beautiful about helicopters. They lack even the rudimentary bird-like grace of an aeroplane. And as they loomed over us, black insects with white search-lights for eyes, startling the birds, I felt only a cold gripping sensation of fear – whilst around me the crowd cheered and cheered. The lady on my left was waving her Falklands souvenir programme and the expression on her face was rapt.

And then the parade itself began. We let one contingent go by and then seven women in front of me turned – arms holding up the banner, quiet, quick and simple. And the crowd went wild. The hard-faced woman beside me lunged for Andrea's piece, screaming, 'I suspected you from the first', pushing and thrusting. We let her through to the barrier. The police grabbed other pieces and stood solid the other side. The man behind us was yelling 'you bastards' and another was screaming about 'our country' and amid all the hubbub I saw your face turn to Karen and I saw tears pouring from your eyes. 'I thought you were my friends! I thought you cared about my son. Don't you dare upset me like this. Don't you dare upset me . . .' Karen was crying too, her back turned to the parade and the policeman shouting over her head, 'Ignore them, ignore them'. And I, forgetting my peace-keeping role, shouting to make my voice heard, said to you, 'We're just as upset as you. It's because we care about your son that we're here!' I wanted to say more, but you turned away to the woman on your other side for comfort, and then a policeman lunged over the barrier at me, hands around my neck, saying, 'Right, you dirty cow, I'm taking you to the police station where scum like you belong.' So I didn't see the rest of the parade, though I know the rest of the women stayed, backs turned and silent to the end.

And of course I didn't see you again. Which was a pity, because we share the same values, you and I. We love freedom, and happiness. Only perhaps you would tell me such things can only be maintained because your son fights to protect them. And I would reply: the fact that he has to fight destroys those things in themselves. I wish there was somewhere we could meet.

# 10
# Who is Breaching the Peace?

What with necessity being the mother of invention and all that . . . we had more or less got ourselves sorted out at the camp. But it was a loose truce between water and women. Improvisation was our salvation. It is amazing what you can live in when you have to!

We had what you might call an 'open plan' kitchen. There was a trestle table, mostly piled up with biscuit tins containing spreads, butter and bread – food for quick snacks. Behind it was a row of plastic bins filled with beans, muesli, tinned food and vegetables. There was an upright kitchen cabinet stacked with coffee, sugar, sauces, herbs and the first aid kit. On a wooden pallet behind the table there were plastic water containers, a plate rack and washing bowls. Several times a day we had to fill the containers with water from the mains supply across the road.

Our 'living-room' was a fire-pit surrounded by straw bales covered in plastic. There was always a kettle perched precariously on the smoking embers and whoever got up first relit the fire each morning. Our office was an old fridge in which we kept the letters to be answered. A chest of drawers contained other handy items like string and paper.

Beyond the kitchen and living-room, stretching down towards the main road, we'd strung a washing line between two trees and draped plastic over it to form a tunnel. Inside the tunnel we'd laid pallets covered with straw. This was the communal bedroom.

As we got more organised and realised that we had overcome the authorities' efforts to wear us down, more women learned the art of building benders camouflaged in the bushes.

At the same time we had some heavy trials ahead of us. In the second week of November supporters began to arrive. On 15 and 16

November, 18 women were to be tried in Newbury Magistrates' Court for the sentry box occupation. The charge was 'behaviour likely to cause a breach of the peace' and we wanted to use the trials effectively to draw the media's attention to our protest and make disarmament a positive election issue. We were being charged under legislation dating back to 1361 and we decided to base our defence on our right to prevent the British and American governments from breaking the terms of the 1969 Genocide Act.

Article II of the Genocide Convention, with which the Act complies, states that

> genocide means any of the following acts committed with intent to destroy, in whole or in part, a national, ethnical, racial or religious group, as such:
> (a) Killing members of the group;
> (b) Causing serious bodily or mental harm to members of the group;
> (c) Deliberately inflicting on the group conditions of life calculated to bring about its physical destruction in whole or in part;
> (d) Imposing measures intended to prevent births within the group;
> (e) Forcibly transferring children of the group to another group.

We asked 'expert' witnesses to testify for the defence that the deployment of Cruise in Europe is an illegal act, by any standard of law.

A local GP, Dr Barbara Cowie, described the effects of a nuclear blast in human terms. She talked of the physical, emotional and psychological devastation that would follow and spread and the way in which any remaining medical services would be rendered completely useless given the extent and enormity of human damage.

E.P. Thompson, a well-known figure in the disarmament campaign, said, 'Our planet is in terrible danger.' He described the environmental consequences and stated that 'damage to the ecosphere, caused by nuclear war, would be unprecedented, therefore nothing in our law books can give us guidance. This unprecedented danger requires unprecedented response.'

The women who stood on trial made their own statements.

*Simone Wilkinson lives with her husband and two children on the Isle of Wight. She had come up with the Welsh women for the action and this was part of her statement to the magistrates:* I can remember meeting a Japanese woman in London while I was expecting my second child. She told me that members of her family were killed in Hiroshima. She said that when a woman was pregnant in Hiroshima, she was given no congratulations but people waited in silence for nine months until the child was born, to see if it was all right.

On 27 August I walked on to the base because I knew a crime was being committed. In 1969 the Genocide Act was passed. It is my opinion that this crime is already being committed . . . the presence of nuclear weapons on our soil is causing serious mental harm to many people . . . women are afraid of having more children.

I personally would like to be at home with my family but I have to be in court. I am on trial for my life, not just for a breach of the peace; but if we lose this case we stand to lose our children.

*Gillian Booth read one of her poems as a statement. This is an extract from it:*

What do you do with someone like me
the animal called human who, all gut, intestines, wings,
flies screaming in the face of official logic
unrepentantly and happily dissident
to join her friends who were occupying that sentry box
at the entrance to this monster
that all my life has breached my peace.
What do you do when I admit that I did nothing wrong
and tell you that after two men got hold of me,
and dragged me back to the gate,
I ran to the side gate laughing,
slid the latch and ran right in again
and that the only way I can be stopped is to silence me by death
for I am the early warning system
because I've seen too much.
What do you do with a revolutionary
who carries no gun
and admits to having fun?

The 18 women were given a choice between 14 days in prison or a bindover for £100 to 'keep the peace' for one year.

On the third day, 17 November, the sewage pipes trial began. We used this case to show that more and more people are being forced to work indirectly for the military machine, because the bulk of our investment (over 40 per cent) is directed towards the arms race and therefore away from more socially useful employment. These are our options – the poverty and stigma of unemployment or the use of our working lives to perpetuate a suicidal economy built on profit from armaments and exploitation of the Third World.

One of the workmen on site that day was called as a witness for our defence. He was asked if he was angry with any of the women and felt they should not have been doing what they did. He replied, 'No, I wasn't angry at all and I wouldn't have reacted violently to any of these women.'

Some women were representing themselves. Helen asked him, 'What kind of work would you like to be doing?'

He said that he did not really want to be involved in work to do with the base and would much rather be building hospitals or houses. But it was clear that this sort of work was not available. Helen made it clear what a farce this all was. She said that this is the twentieth century, the nuclear age, and yet we are brought before a court using laws written in the fourteenth century which have no relevance at all to the present situation. She said to the magistrates, 'You are making a mockery of the law, this court, and the word "peace".'

*Charlie nervously approached the witness box. In a clear, strong voice she read her statement:* 'It is time the magistrates, police and workmen at the base at USAF Greenham Common took responsibility for their actions. Most of the workmen that I have spoken to say they don't agree with nuclear weapons but that they are just doing their job; that if they left that job they would become unemployed. If we didn't spend such atrocious amounts of money on weapons that are supposedly never to be used, there would be jobs for us all, better education, better national health service. We would be a prosperous country. The people who continue to carry out their jobs – working on the base, arresting women and sentencing them – are contributing to the perpetuation of nuclear war . . .

'I resent the fact that people in positions of power can break the law, causing a breach of the peace, by planning to mass murder. And yet I have been trying to prevent this from happening and have been arrested for it.'

*Katrina Howse had been involved with the camp since its early
days and with other women had started a camp outside RAF
Waddington, now the largest nuclear weapons store in Britain. She
addressed her statement directly to the magistrates:* '. . . What are
you doing to keep the peace? The power you are using is supporting
nuclear weapons. It supports binding women's voices, binding our
minds and bodies in prison so our voices cannot be heard. So our
warning of Death is being repressed.

'But we cannot be silenced. And I cannot be bound over. I am
asking you to keep the peace . . . We are not on trial . . . you are.'

All this was lost on the magistrates, however, who turned a deaf
ear to the moral arguments, the eloquent speeches of the defence
lawyer, the powerful statements of the women and the courageous
evidence of some workmen. Like finely tuned robots they sentenced woman after woman to prison. Supporters in court were
naturally appalled at the injustice and cried 'Shame' and 'Have
courage to do the right thing' as the women were led away.

The 11 women in this trial were given the same sentence as those
in the previous trial. As a result of the two trials, 6 women chose to
be bound over and 23 went to prison: for all of them it was their first
time. Twelve women were taken to East Sutton Park women's
prison in Kent and 11 went to Drake Hall women's prison in
Staffordshire.

*Charlie*: After being led from court we were taken back to the
police station where we had to go through documentation –
property sorted out, forms signed and we were searched. Finally at
7 o'clock our group left. As we were going north we realised we
were going to Drake Hall, an 'open' prison.

After a long, tiring journey up the M5 we finally arrived. I peered
out, trying to see what it looked like in the dark. I could make out
flat buildings: it didn't look like a prison at all. There weren't any
big walls surrounding it, only a small hedge – no sign of barbed
wire. It had the appearance of a mental institution.

We saw the prison doctor who asked us if we had ever attempted
suicide, if we'd ever taken drugs. He looked at our arms to check
for needle marks. He felt us to see if we were pregnant. We were
weighed and stripped.

*Carmel McConnell was also taken to Drake Hall. She had come*

82

*from Brighton to join in the sentry box action. While she was in prison she wrote a diary on bits of toilet paper and smuggled it out in her socks:* Upon our arrival, a big strong-looking prison officer said, 'There's two ways of doing your time with us in Drake Hall – the easy way or the hard way.'

I wanted to say something profound and strengthening in reply, but all that we five managed was some nervous laughter and many comments like, 'So where's the restaurant in this holiday camp?'

*Wednesday 17 November* – Our first full day here has been alternately bizarrely humorous, and quite grim. Spent the morning scrubbing floors with carbolic soap, till we were seen by the Governor. She's trying hard to sound benevolent at the same time as telling us that we're not getting any remission, nor numbers, and that we won't be considered as real inmates. Most important thing is that the women in here know something about us and have been coming up to us with newspaper cuttings about Greenham. One woman lent us her radio so that we could hear the news, and an MP has asked a question about us in the House of Commons.

The only crime that women in here have committed is that of not having enough money and influence to escape conviction.

Women are magic. We've been singing a lot, and the women in here don't seem to dislike us, so that's OK.

Back to the bog roll tomorrow!

*Thursday 18th* – At lunchtime we found out that Gill is in lock-up (Allen House, they call it a 'segregation unit', and they use it for punishing women who do naughty things like persistently walking on the grass or refusing to work). She'd been put there for refusing to work, so we had a quick gathering and decided we'd stop working on Monday, but then we changed to an immediate refusal.

We had been asked to go to Stafford Police Station to be fingerprinted and photographed, but we refused and they eventually backed down. They weren't too pleased with us and got even more displeased with our refusing to work. The Governor told us that we'd be working against the 'community' by refusing to work, and she's told Claire and Katrina that they're cranks and megalomaniacs.

Good news is that Liz has got some real toothpaste, rather than prison tooth powder, and that a woman who's being released tomorrow is letting us give her a message to smuggle out.

New bog roll tomorrow.

*Friday 19th* – Today's been busy. Went to the gym this morning, but just before the game of basketball got going, two big strong women came and took us to Allen House.

We were told to write a defence and I put down some heart-warming stuff, asking why we should assist in the smooth running of an institution designed to facilitate our punishment, and that of other equally innocent women. I read this to the Governor and now I'm in lock-up for three days. What fun.

Got loads of letters and two bouquets each. We haven't got any vases, so we've put the flowers into our potty.

*I get a visit tomorrow!!!*


*Charlie*: On Friday the 12 of us were all put into Allen House for refusing to work. As there were only six cells we completely occupied the punishment block and consequently prevented other women from being punished. We were locked up for most of the day except when we had exercise in the yard where we did karate exercises Carmel taught us. Food was brought into the cells and from 6.45 a.m. bedding and mattresses were taken out of the cell for maximum discomfort until 5 p.m.

Being in the punishment block was an effective protest but it meant that we were no longer able to communicate with other women. It was also very boring and cold. The hours dragged on, visits were the most important time of the day. As civil prisoners we could have a visit every day for 15 minutes. We were visited mainly by local supporters and people from the vigil set up outside the prison since our arrival, but women from the camp and relatives also came. Before a visit we were searched, and during the visit eating and drinking were forbidden. You could smoke however, as long as they were cigarettes and not roll-ups.


*Carmel: Saturday 20th* – Not feeling too cheerful today. Scrubbed our cells this morning, it's OK for us to keep ourselves clean, otherwise other women would have to do more work. Then, after lunch Kathy, Helen, Katrina and I were told we could have our visit. Heart leaps out of body.

Laura and Rhona were sitting in a long room, surrounded by big strong women in blue. I tried to sound comfortable and cool during the visit, but my heart was going mad, pulse leaping out on to the table. Had a little cry afterwards, but feeling OK now, just tired of it and feeling powerless to thank everyone for their support. Nine days left.

*Sunday 21st* – Another thrilling day. During our daily hour of exercise in the yard we did a warm-up that I used to do for karate, trust games, and lots of singing. We were given a lot of food today for some reason. Wonder what's in it.

Really nice woman on duty this evening, has asked us if we're bored, says that she at least has got her knitting! We reminded her that we at least are leaving here soon.

Three women escaped today, and more can't be punished because we've filled up the punishment area. *Good*.

While these women were in prison, the lines of communication and support inside and outside continued. Mary recorded some of this in the Camp Day Book:

*Tuesday 23rd* – Io and I got up early today to visit Mandy and others at East Sutton Park prison. Got news that Arlene has started a peace camp of 100 women outside Drake Hall. Also that Reagan is renaming the MX missile 'The Peacemaker'! Caught the 10 a.m. coach to Maidstone, ate some junk food and found a bus to Sutton Valence. The wind was whistling through the pines as we arrived at the white gates of the prison and tottered up the curving drive. We rang and waited, as requested, and a woman welcomed us in and scrutinised our visiting order. We were ushered into a room with beautiful Jacobean carving, and a very nasty photo of the queen.

Then – a violent explosion at the door! Mandy pushed past the large, authoritarian woman with the keys and threw herself at us, literally. My teeth were nearly knocked out, but it was good to see her looking perfectly well and happy. Rebecca popped her head in but was removed. I shouted her name and was asked not to. Shortly afterwards the door opened again and Rebecca charged in, officially this time. She had successfully worn down the authorities and got her own way. Good for her! Mandy says a group of Manchester prostitutes will be joining us on 12 December . . . our circle is widening. Fences between women are being broken down.

*Charlie*: On Wednesday Kath and I came out of the punishment block and agreed to work. We were going insane in Allen House. At one stage I rocked on my bed for hours and Kath jumped up and down on hers. I felt all right about this decision because I thought it important to challenge the system that put me in prison for trying to alert people about the threat to their future, only up to the point of causing myself harm.

That day was thoroughly enjoyable. I put in a governor's application to move into the same room as Kath. (To do anything or enquire about anything you have to fill in a form and post it in the letter box of your house.) It was decided that I could. I put my big bouquet of flowers from Camden Council into the rubbish bin with some water and arranged all the cards I had received on the top of the wardrobe. Although we had agreed to work we only did about 20 stitches of a purse between us. Gym is compulsory for the first five days on entering Drake Hall, so Kath and I went to the gym where we played basketball most of the day. We brought coffee and sugar, it seemed like luxury compared to Allen House.

The rest of the women remained inside Allen House until Friday, being cheered up by women shouting their support from the main prison. They communicated with each other by shouting through the pipe-holes at the back of their cells; and from the picket outside the prison gates the sounds of drumming and sometimes of women keening, filtered through to women in the cells.

*Charlie*: At 6 o'clock on Friday morning, without warning, we were all transferred to different prisons. The newspapers reported the Home Office saying that 'we were a disruptive influence'. Considering we had little contact with other women, being in Allen House, I don't think we could be accused of incitement. The only reason I can think of for our transfer is that we were preventing other women from being punished by completely occupying the punishment block. It surprised us and we were frustrated at having been moved so early in the morning, not having the chance to say goodbye to everyone.

We were driven out by the back entrance of the prison so that the vigil wouldn't see us leave, then on to the motorway heading south with a police escort in front and behind. It was very disconcerting speeding down a motorway without the slightest idea where we were being taken. As we neared the outskirts of London the van behind suddenly disappeared. We knew we were going to Holloway. The other van took three women to Styal women's prison in Cheshire and four women to Crookham Wood prison in Kent. The solicitors had to be informed of our whereabouts and by Saturday there were people maintaining a vigil outside Holloway.

*Carmel*: The days in Holloway were fine, the nights a bit scary in a cell all by myself. We were on a wing with 'short stay' women, mainly inside for non-payment of fines. Those women really taught us a lot about how our activities in the peace movement look to the 'ordinary women' outside, coping with endless pressures, no money, etc. They thought we were a bit mad to consider doing the same actions after being released, but they were warm and honest, and we didn't find anyone who still thought we were wrong once they'd chatted to us and discussed how we'd got into doing direct action and why.

*Charlie*: Holloway is built on three descending levels lower than the surrounding buildings. A tall, curvy, red-brick wall forms a circular barrier around the prison. The new buildings look very smart and the grounds are beautiful with flowers, bushes and trees. Walking around the prison one just can't imagine the horrors that occur within.

Inside, women are confined to a wing and only come out for exercise (walking around a yard for half an hour), to see the doctor, to go to church or to work. You're locked up most of the time in your cell except for two hours in the evening in the association room of the wing. I spent most of the day looking out of the window (they used to be glass but too often they were smashed by women wanting to cut their wrists). It was difficult to talk to the other women on the wing. One woman who was in a cell next to me insisted that 'we were all dead and there ain't any nuclear bombs'. She made me laugh, however, although it was sad to see her in the state she was in. She seemed a harmless old woman. When I asked her what she had done, she replied that she'd stolen ten teddy bears. During the night she would sing pop songs to me.

It was very depressing. The food was awful and I didn't want to eat it, but meals in prison are social events and the next thing to look forward to in the day. It was very difficult to sleep as women would scream constantly through the night, or they would bang the windows for hours on end. I felt helpless, I had to try and ignore their desperate screams.

I was very glad when Tuesday morning came. At 5 o'clock I was woken by a bang on the cell door and a shout, 'Get up, you're going home'. I dressed quickly and stripped the bed. I had become very protective towards my tiny little space and resented the warders opening the cell door and coming in. The thought of freedom was very scary. So many things to do, so many things that would happen the first day out, not to mention the press.

The screws, as I now called them, didn't come for an hour. That hour was torture. I walked up and down my cell, I couldn't wait any longer. I had to go through the whole discharge system, another strip search – but, at least, the last. Then I walked through the two iron gates and out of the prison. I was taken aback, there was a huge crowd waiting for us to come out and they were cheering. The noise echoed around in my head. I knew I had to walk on to meet them. I couldn't go back now, could I? Then all at once I had microphones, champagne, sweet bars, flowers, cameras, kisses and hugs thrust at me. I tried to answer questions as clearly as possible and return people's delight in seeing me, but I was happy.

# 11
# You Are Surrounded

Only two weeks to go till 12 December! There were still loads of things to be done, marquees to hire, a booklet to prepare, meetings to speak at. We still had no idea of how many women would come, but the embrace the base idea had generated lots of excitement. Surrounding the Cruise missile base had different meanings for different people. It represented women joining together by linking hands which would both contain the evil within the base and surround it with positive healing energy. We were to transform the fence from its negative, destructive purpose into a gallery of women's work. The fence was to show what was at stake for all of us threatened by nuclear war. We also felt our women's energy would make a difference to the military potency of the base. Psychically we wanted to weaken the fence as a barrier but we didn't know how this would work as we had no plans to pull it down. Nor did we.

Men kept saying, 'What can we do to help?' and women were asking, 'Can I bring my husband?' Repeating time after time, 'This is a women's action' and having to explain why we felt it was so important for women to take the initiative. Coming up against blank stares, barbed criticism, justifying . . . always having to justify.

Why do we always have to fight for the right to organise for ourselves as women?

Meetings at the camp, huddled together around the fire, fingers blue with cold trying to hold a pen to make notes of what has to be done. Must have water at every gate. We need containers. How will we get it there? What about signs? Someone has to drive round and see how many we need. It's raining, where can we paint them? Under the carport at Barbara's house. Need brushes, paint, boards. Candles. We must have candles to light in the evening. How about torches? We could have a torch-making workshop for the men.

89

What about the men? Maybe they can walk to Aldermaston while women are encircling the base. Have the men's support group got the creche organised?

We need food at each gate. And toilets . . . who's organising that? Can we get toilets for disabled women?

More meetings . . . the rain is bucketing down. Holding each other, sharing umbrellas around the fire or squashed into Io's van, women spilling out the door. Rumours that the Socialist Workers Party are going to try and break the circle. What do we do? We'll just have to play it by ear. Deborah's phone is ringing nonstop in London. Angela's phone is just as bad in Newbury.

It's 9 December and we're starting to get an inkling that maybe, just maybe, we'll get enough women to surround the base. What about the police? We'll have to at least speak to them about traffic arrangements. Aggie and Barbara go to see the local superintendent, map in hand with suggestions on how to direct the traffic. Aggie is Bridget Evans, Barbara becomes Brenda Evans. We agree to paint our signs to a one-way system. The police are polite but cagey. 'You haven't got permission to hold this demonstration you know.' 'Oh well, it's a bit late to worry about that now. Here's the map we've made of the perimeter fence and roads. We'd appreciate your co-operation with the traffic.'

Last minute panics!

We need seeds to distribute into and around the base, symbols of life. A carload of women rush off to Oxford.

The company hiring the marquees has backed out with the excuse that it's an illegal demo. Phone calls all over southern England. We at least have to have a creche tent! Bridget Evans is appearing everywhere. She locates marquees in Gloucester on Friday night. Saturday morning we leave in the removals van for a hair-raising drive to get them back by nightfall.

There aren't enough pallets. The mud is knee deep in places. There isn't enough firewood and pallets are being broken up to burn. We need straw bales for ground covering inside the marquees. More trips in the van to a local farmer, haggling, the price goes up because it's us – but his conscience gets the better of him.

It's Saturday evening, 11 December, and the last marquee is dropped off. The Woodcraft Folk are erecting the tents at the Orange Gate, women are erecting them at other gates around the base. New women are arriving, we're exhausted but feverish with excitement. Friendships are forming as the new arrivals help with the marquees or form huddled groups around fires. It's late and we finally crawl, eyes heavy, bodies drained, into damp sleeping bags in the marquees or under plastic makeshift shelters.

*Chris Mulvey was one of the women who responded to our call. She came from Dublin, Ireland: One call for 16,000 women to join an action at the base on 12 December 1982 resulted in 30,000 women arriving.*

There it was in front of me: the fence, three times as tall as I and stretching further than my eye could see. I wanted to decorate it. I wanted to fill its holes with colour and with life, to transform it, so that when I looked again I would see Life and Beauty not threat and cold sterility.

But I had nothing. All around me women were at work. With bits of wool and twine tying up balloons and posters, sticking babies' clothing, photos of their children and pictures of their loved ones into the coldness of its wire. I was standing in a mass of knotted bramble. Grass, weed and gorse, intertwined, were growing live up to the fence. How wonderful to fill its holes with this. So strong the wish to make my contribution, to fill that fence with Life and yet somehow I could not do it. A spirit stronger than my own desire and taking hold of me said, No: to tear a single blade of grass is violation.

And so I took a pen and on some paper drew a flower to stick into the fence to represent the earth that I had come here to defend.

I hadn't planned to come. I knew about it but I had excuses. Wanting to play some part, I went along to Trinity where the Irish women were preparing for the weekend. I listened to them speak of why they were going, of their fears and hopes and anxieties, of their inspiration. And for the first time what was to happen many times that weekend happened: from somewhere a spirit rose and flowing through my veins drowned out all other words and thoughts. With a certainty unusual to me I simply knew I had to go. And so I went, for a hundred different reasons, for the earth, for the children, for the Greenham women, for peace and for the Spirit that had overtaken me. I knew nothing except that nuclear war was wrong and here was a chance for me to say no.

The next morning after a long and thoughtful ride we came to Greenham. My conversation ebbed as the miles of fencing began. Inside just flat, grey, dead cement; outside the damp scented

91

greenery of a misty morning countryside. There was an aura about the place that was not limited by the fence. A greyness that was not mist, a silence that was not full, a strength that was brutal rather than reassuring. My excitement hiccoughed as I caught a glimpse of what I was choosing to oppose.

Once down from the bus and surrounded by working women the spirit of the peace camp rather than the military camp seemed to be the more real. There was nobody giving orders or telling us what to do. We'd each had a message from the Greenham women, to bring a hymn to express why we were here and that was all. The rest was left to us, and somehow through an intuition or a mysterious unspoken understanding, there was no conflict, there was no breakdown in communication, there was no paralysis of action.

The tents were put up, the tea was made, the fence was decorated and transformed from a sterile ugliness into a dancing work of art. At night especially was this obvious. The darkness hid the fence and as we walked about the base, the light from our candles lit up only our symbols and there, five feet above the ground, all around the base, was a women's collage of life.

Sometime during that day we joined hands and began to sing. Hand in hand in hand, for nine miles we formed a living chain to lock in the horrors of war, to stand between them and our world and to say: we will meet your violence with a loving embrace, for it is the surest way of defusing it. How strong I felt when I joined my voice to the waves of voices shouting Freedom and when the echoes from so far away drifted across the base to my ears. I took my seeds and wrapped them in mud and with all the love and strength I felt threw them inside the fence: Take root and grow. Tell them that life will prevail and that in the midst of ugliness beauty can flourish.

I saw again the web, the symbol of the Greenham women, woven in wool, into the fence and on to the grass, drawn on posters and on garments. Everywhere the web, and questions of its meaning were stilled as somehow from within the understanding grew. We are all interdependent, we are all responsible for each other, how delicate the strands, how strong the web. The ancient spider goddess weaving tirelessly the web of life, again and again and again, as often as it is needed. Never stopping, never hesitating, working tirelessly to build again what was broken or torn or damaged.

With wool, with homespun inner knowledge, we will weave again the strands of true existence. We will remove whatever lies of force and violence have got caught. We will unravel them and weave again where holes were torn, until with truth and love and gentleness the web is whole and strong.

By 6.30 the next day our action had begun. Joined by other women we sat down in front of our gate, huddling close to keep out the cold, talking almost in whispers, and taking turns to sip tea from crooked paper cups rescued from the fence the night before. Anticipation crackled in the air like the walkie-talkie messages that joined us to the other gates. Cars passed. The odd policeman, rigid and unsmiling, and vanloads of women waving and laughing. Inside the base there was no movement, no sound. It was as though the world had paused. A question hung in the air. No one knew what was going to happen.

At 7.30 the police arrived. A song began as more vans drew up and suddenly police were everywhere. Inside the fence and outside, more and more arrived. They began to remove the women. I watched as friends were dragged along the road and flung into the mud at the side of the banks. The clash between women and police began in earnest now. It terrified me. There was fear and violence in the air, shouts and cries, harsh orders and banshee wailing, a woman's scream and the thud of bodies flung on to the mud. Behind the fence a woman fell to the ground and two policemen rushed towards her. One, twisting his fingers into her hair, began to drag her through the gate. I saw his boot and heard the thud and suddenly I had to vomit. Police were dragging, shoving, pulling, but women kept returning. Stronger now and even more determined. The fear was gone. Through chant and song we inspired each other and expressed our message. Again they were dragged away and this time some bikes and vans got through. Anger choked and sorrow tasted bitter as I saw the gates opening to let them in. In shrieks and wails I flung my hatred at the swarming men. Wanting so much to stop them, wanting so much to win . . . until I saw in amazement the women returning again to the road. And I began to understand.

In their hundreds, arm in arm and singing, they were lying and sitting now in front of buses. The sun began to shine.

Confidence and strength were growing. While the police stood in groups waiting for orders, women all round me were laughing! We were singing songs of peace, songs of joy, songs of courage. Women were feeding each other, hugging each other, crying in each others' arms, strengthening each other with word and with song. Women were talking to the police, reminding them that we were on their side. Peace descended almost tangibly. There was a luminous

93

moment when I understood what I have believed for a long time: Gentleness is stronger than force. They did not win. They could not win, for they could not stop us dreaming. They could not stop us saying no. They could not stop the spirit.

Our action lasted nearly six hours. Though the blockade continued at the other gates, we could not join them, as we had a boat to catch. I left Greenham still possessed by its spirit. Even now the spirit is with me. I believe in the power of women, I believe in the wisdom of women, I believe in the vision of women. And because I am a woman I am responsible.

Like the spider goddess, I will weave with you the threads of our existence, human, animal, and plant together. I will bind them with truth and love and gentleness. Together, strong enough to overcome all lies and violence, we will build again a web of life. Tirelessly, as often as is needed, again and again and again . . .

After everyone had gone home we were left feeling totally drained. The number of women who had responded to our call and the powerful emotions generated by those two days had overwhelmed us.

*Jayne*: After 12 December the whole of the nine-mile fence was covered with women's work. For a few days very little was touched but then 'they' began to take it down. The 'they' were a variety of people – MOD, soldiers, the Newbury Anglo-American Friendship group and groups of local people who on request volunteered to remove the banners, photos, children's toys, women's artwork, webs, etc. These groups of people included children. It was incredibly sad to see pictures of little children taking the things off the fence in the local paper. The people and the newspapers who think they are pro-nuclear, pro-Cruise, described the women's work as 'debris', 'rubbish', 'mess'. I suppose they had to try and see it like this to do what they were doing. So they went out with their black plastic rubbish bags and stuffed them full of the amazing collection of things left by the 30,000 women.

My goddess, that fence – what we did to that fence! What we did to that artificial boundary around the once common land, the place that was once covered with golden gorse, trees, and wildlife, that land that once belonged to the people, the animals, the trees and plants. That land that was sold to the military who covered it with concrete and made a dream into a nightmare.

I saw a small group of men and boys working their way towards the camp, so I took a chair and a couple of tangerines to where they had to pass before they got to the main gate. I sat quietly, eating tangerines and watching them. Opposite me were pictures, baby clothes and a hank of real, black hair. The men and boys looked self-conscious, as well they might. They tore the things from the fence; the black hair went quickly into the bag. They had small, sharp blades that they slashed at the wool and ribbon. I felt sorry for the boys and angry at the men who 'led' the group.

When they got past the main gate and into the camp I found myself walking towards them. It was as if this was the last desecration, the last straw, and they shouldn't be allowed to just do it without feeling something. Other women who were around were also drawn to them. It seemed that they were being so disrespectful to all the women who were there on 12 December.

We didn't touch them but we stood in their way. We put our faces close to the things on the fence that they slashed at with their sharp blades. Some women held on to banners and were dragged with them along the ground.

'Do you want police assistance?' the MOD asked them.

'No,' they said but looked very shaken.

We whispered into their ears, we stood close behind them so they could feel our presence, our breath. A deaf woman hissed the word 'Hex' at them. We women, with no words, were in full communication with each other. I remember two women who were visiting, standing in their skirts and makeup – their arms outstretched, backs against the fence touching a spray of flowers, a child's well-used toy, a family photograph. They looked the men steadily in the eye and told them that the women who put the things there wanted peace.

The fence was almost bare again – cold, bare, alien – but still vibrating with energy.

*Women occupy sentry box, 27 August 1982*

*MOD reclaim telephone extension*

*September 1982 – 'You can take away our structures but you can't evict our spirit'*

*'I can't find the instructions for unwinding this, guv.' Sewage pipes action, 5 October 1982*

*Home improvements: building a 'bender' extension after*
*September 1982 eviction*

*Decorating the fence on December 12th – 'tea break'*

*December 12th – encircling the base*

*Post December 12th chaos*

*Dawn dance on the silos, 1st January 1983*

*Green gate camp – privacy amidst the chaos*

*Digging a Greenham garden at the Main gate*

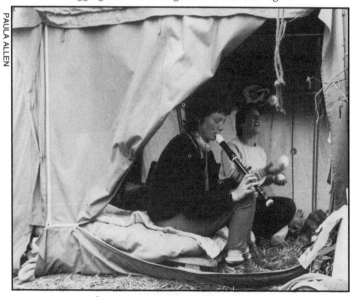

*Creative pastimes – 'who needs tv?'*

EVA GRAPE

*Police and bailiffs seize personal property – women assert their rights. Eviction, May 12 1983*

EVA GRAPE

*Heavy-handed police*

*Post-eviction blues*

*The heart of the camp – the camp fire*

*Transforming metal – 29 October 1983*

*Taking down the barriers – 29 October 1983*

*Main gate, February 1984*

# 12
# Overcoming Barriers

The next few months were an intense succession of events, actions, confusion. So much happened. Hundreds of women visiting for a day, staying a while or coming to live at the camp. Always new faces, strange faces. We had become the 'front-line' focus of a burgeoning political movement that was growing by the day.

It was a kind of crash course in reality – suddenly all the pain, anger and injustice of women's experience was flooding into our lives. We were finding our problems mirrored in all the women around us.

We were women from all classes, all walks of life, and the pattern was emerging clearly. Was the issue that clear-cut? Was our greatest enemy Cruise missiles or were nuclear weapons only part of a much bigger evil?

There were warning voices from veterans of long-waged campaigns. 'We must define our prime aims, we must state our position clearly.' But we could no longer ignore our personal histories and the way they revealed the enormity of what we were up against.

Over the next few weeks, with the constant flow of visitors and large numbers of new longer-term campers, communications between us began to break down. We spent half our time just trying to cope with the more immediate demands and the other half hidden in our benders recovering from exhaustion. The most pressing demands were public relations and information to visitors or to public meetings. We had requests for speakers every day of the week.

Then there was the press. 'How long have you been here? Where do you get your water from? How many times have you been arrested? Where do you shit? What about your family? Why is it women only? Why do you think you'll be more effective than the 60s protests? We've avoided war for 37 years, why do you think we won't avoid it for another 40 years?'

Day after day the same questions. The reports were printed, our answers were often twisted or edited out . . . we were naïve, well-intentioned but emotional and woolly-minded. We weren't supposed to show emotion.

Cold, cold mornings, muddy slush in and over everything. Limp teabags, damp sugar, the fire's out. Layer upon layer of clothing and still the cold and damp penetrated to our bones.

'Hello, how long have you been here?' says a reporter. You look up and there's a film crew, camera lenses watching you as you stumble, bleary-eyed, trying to get the fire going for your first cup of tea.

'Look, do you think you could make another cup of tea but this time bring it over here,' he points to a soggy, plastic-covered hay bale.

'Hang on. What's the issue here?' you wonder. 'Is it our domestic habits or Cruise missiles?'

A car pulls up and a couple get out. They approach nervously. 'Umm, we've brought you some wood and a couple of sleeping bags.' Wonderful people. Without their support it would have been unbearable.

While all this disruption was going on, an impetus was already moving us towards another action – for us the most daring and frightening action we had, until then, attempted.

There had still been no real public debate – attention was constantly being drawn away from the stated purpose of the camp to our domestic lives. We wanted to take the focus back where it belonged – inside the base.

*Eleanor McManus is a working-class woman from Glasgow and she'd come to Greenham a few months earlier. She was one of the women who inspired many others to cross that wire-mesh barrier:* I had made a decision that I wanted to enter the base and attempt to go on top of the silos, but at this time my thoughts were incomplete as I had no idea of how this could be achieved. Time had been passing very quickly and suddenly it was Christmas, leading up to the new year, and I had done nothing constructive. Christmas was chaotic, women everywhere, but no time to plan, discuss, work through fears . . . Oh, no, I thought, this will never happen!

Skeeter and Ceri got involved at this time and I began to feel more relaxed . . . maybe, just maybe it'll happen after all.

After hours of discussion between us and a few other women, Ceri, Skeeter and I decided it was time we went round to the silo area. It was dark, scary and very quiet. We were beginning to get very nervous and, worst of all, we realised that not one of us even knew what a silo looked like. After two hours of tripping over bushes we decided to go back and look for a picture of a silo.

Ceri found a photograph in a book and off we went again, hoping to find a silo.

After all this, we realised that the building we'd been staring at a hundred yards inside the fence had to be it!

Next night, back to the silos yet again. We decided to let everybody know what was going on, open it up for discussion.

From then on it was three meetings a day, every day. New women arriving, every meeting repeating the same story time and time again. Feeling drained, lacking energy, kept going. Fears being aired, feeling confused – was it going to happen? Getting stroppy, leaving meetings, getting upset. Feels like hitting my head against a brick wall. Why do I set myself up as a target? This is becoming group therapy, I don't like it. Walked away, came back.

Things beginning to change . . . down to practicalities, long discussion. Was cutting the fence violent? Yes! No! Yes! . . . getting nowhere.

'Is there another way? What about ladders, is it possible?'

'How high is the fence? Can we go over?'

'Yes.'

Right! Got to get ladders. Phew! at least that's settled.

What's next? Time.

'How about midnight, be in there at the beginning of the new year?'

'Not practical.'

'Why?'

'Not enough light, press won't be able to film. We need the press for protection.'

'Well then, has anybody any other time in mind?'

'What about dawn?'

Sounds good. Yes, dawn it is.

Beginning to feel good, things getting together.

Now that's settled, what will we wear?

'Do we want to wear bright colours so they'll know it's us?'

'Why?'

'Well they might have guns.'

Oh shit, here we go again.

'What if they shoot?'

'They won't.'

'They might.'

'Well we've got to take that chance.'

Eventually we decided on a bib with a luminous, painted womyn's symbol on front and back.

It's finally coming together. Now to buy the materials. How we managed this I'll never know. We decided we had to be discreet, buy one ladder in each store. Of course this never happened. What we ended up doing was buying ten ladders in one shop and walking down Reading high street carrying three ladders apiece balanced on our heads. How the authorities never caught on through all of this I don't know.

At last it is 31 December, New Year's Eve. Some women went to see the press that day, having phoned them in advance with the cryptic request, 'We'd like to discuss with you your coverage of Greenham for the coming year . . . today.' The conversation with journalists went something like this. 'We want reporters at Greenham at 6 o'clock in the morning.' Most of them shook their heads and said, 'You're not going to get people out at that hour, not unless you're going to go into the base.'

The women would clear their throats, 'Could you close that door for a minute, please . . . well, as a matter of fact . . .'

In the evening a group of uninvited press turned up at the camp with the idea of filming a New Year's Eve party at Greenham. Well, a party was the furthest thing from our minds, but we didn't want to jeopardise the action, so . . . we staged a little party for them. Eventually, after filming our slightly forced jollity, they left.

Late that night six women crept through the woods from the Blue Gate to hide the ladders in the bracken. A few women slept in the woods that night, the rest of them, at least 50, crammed into Barbara's house. At the house it was frenetic but purposeful.

*Eleanor*: Got to get down to practicalities. Who's doing legal observing? Have you got everyone's name and address? Everybody talking at once, getting nowhere fast. At this point I couldn't take any more and decided to go back to camp. Wanted to phone my mum, couldn't get through, feeling frustrated, angry. I walked back to camp, a beautiful night, quiet and calm. I relaxed and enjoyed the journey. Before going to bed I shouted to the women at the fire, 'Will somebody wake me up? I'm in the green tent behind the bushes in the small clearing.' I said goodnight and off I went.

6 a.m. Barbara's house. It's pitch black outside. Inside the house women waking, nerves raw, the tension is at screaming point but everyone is containing it . . . we have to be silent.

The first vanload goes off to the base. The van is back again, more women creeping, stumbling, 'Shh, don't wake the neighbours,' out of the house into the van.

*Bee Burgess was at art college before coming to the camp. She had arrived at the base earlier and now, as dawn was approaching, she was getting impatient:* The sky would be lighting at 7.30 and not all the women had arrived. We wait, nerves tender, excitement spinning through our bodies . . . at last everyone is here. The ladders are found, we discard their camouflage and start moving towards the fence. The silos loom threateningly in the half-light of dawn. We knew that now, standing before the fence, we would need to be so quick. Two ladders are propped successfully against the fence, with carpet laid over the top barbed wire, and another ladder is dropped down the other side. The atmosphere is frantic.

There is a flash of light from behind us, an over-zealous reporter more concerned for his story than for our safety and the success of our action. We start clambering over. There are headlights coming towards us from inside the base while it seems like an endless stream of women are crossing the barriers of destruction. As we jump from the ladders on the other side, we crouch for a moment, waiting for the other women, wondering, 'Will we get there?' In the next second we've joined hands – suddenly two policemen are there, aggressively shoving the ladders and wrenching them away from the inside of the fence, leaving two women on top of the barbed wire . . . they jump . . . we begin singing and walking quickly, almost at a run, towards the silos. Our hearts are beating and our voices ring out clearly . . . the sky is light and it's raining softly on our faces.

We scrambled up the mud-drenched slopes to the top of the silos. Unbelieving – but knowing – we cheered, waved, jumped up and down, hugged each other in what seemed like an endless amount of energy! We had brought with us a huge piece of cloth with 'Peace 83' painted across it which we held for the women to see, for the TV cameras who would then take it back to broadcast into living rooms all over the country. For an hour we danced, sang and made women's peace symbols with the stones that lay on the surface. We saw police and American military buses arriving. We sat in a large circle and one by one we were dragged down the muddy slopes into the buses and driven to Newbury police station where we were eventually charged with 'breach of the peace' – we had been prepared for the possibility of being charged under the Official Secrets Act . . . but it would appear that the MOD didn't want to involve themselves.

Still our energy continued to vibrate in our feelings and voices throughout the police cells.


*Inside the green tent at the main gate, Eleanor was waking from a deep sleep:* I opened my eyes. It was light! Half-dressed, I stuck my head out of the tent. A woman was walking past and I asked her the time.

'Eight forty-five,' she replied.

'Oh no,' I screamed. 'I don't believe it.'

Tears were streaming, I didn't know how to cope. I had just seen a dream disappear in front of me . . . but it wasn't quite like that somehow. Jill appeared, saw me and exclaimed, 'Eleanor! What are you doing here?'

'I overslept,' I said. 'What happened? I want to know.'

'They got in, 44 women! Eleanor, they made it!' She was ecstatic. 'But how did you sleep in?'

I was crying, 'I don't know, I don't know.'

Jill took me to her tent, we were both crying. 'Do you feel as though something has been taken from you?' she asked.

'I don't know . . . I feel sad but I feel good, I think. They made it! Jill, it happened!'

More tears. How am I going to get through this day?

In the late afternoon, I went to the house. The phone rang – it was Mandy calling from Reading nick. Her first question was to ask me how I was.

'I should be asking you that,' I said. We both laughed.

I went through so many things that day, but what was so important to me was that I was given space and support to do this by loving, caring friends around me.

And most important of all – we had done it. The fence was no longer a barrier, and that made us want to get into the base more often. We thought of different ways of going in. We'd used ladders to climb over the fence – why couldn't we slide under it too . . . like snakes? This inspired us to explore snake mythology.

The serpent periodically sheds its skin, freeing itself from its constricting, outgrown casement by undergoing a frenzied 'dance of death' in which it wriggles free. So the snake represents psychological renewal, the change from winter to spring and reincarnation. In some places the serpent is shown swallowing its own tail, indicating the circle of Eternity; the beginninglessness and endlessness of life. The 'wisdom of the serpent' is suggested by its ever-watchful, lidless eyes. Our historical fascination with snakes comes from our secret wish to grasp full knowledge of the world which we cannot find in waking-day consciousness alone. But the snake sees all. The mythical dragon was a serpent, too. She is a creature that has grown in power and wisdom by shedding all constricting ideas and attitudes.

We also began thinking about the practical implications of 'snakes and ladders'. We decided to spread an invitation to women to come and camp anywhere round the base, to snake under or climb over the fence. This also suggested a practical solution for our community's internal problems, a way of providing more space, of spreading out and breaking up into smaller, workable groups.

At the end of January a group of women set up a new camp in the woods at the Green Gate. Among them was *Lisa Tide, a German woman who had moved to Greenham in December '82:* At the Green Gate there was space again for us to weave webs, to sing and keen and for rituals to reconnect ourselves to mother earth: we cast healing spells over the mistreated common. I planted a herb garden with a few perennial plants, for me so much a sign of the future, healing plants. And we began to hold vigils at the gate when the construction workers came to work each morning.

It was also meant to be a place of retreat, where you could kiss your lover or scream out your anger without visitors being upset and press picking on you to find something to get away from the subject of Cruise missiles. It was a perfect place for children to play, a sort of ideal adventure playground, but more real because it becomes home.

On 7 February we had our first 'snake' action. We made three long cloth snakes and inside each of them were 30 women. Michael Heseltine, the Secretary of State for Defence, was visiting Newbury and we decided to mark his visit by demonstrating the ease with which we (and anyone else) could infiltrate the base.

Over 100 women undid some bolts in the fence and entered the base undetected. One of the snakes succeeded in weaving its way from one end of the base to the other before being rounded up and bussed out.

# 13
# Punishment is Political

Excitement was building again, our thoughts and energy were now turning towards the next big court case. Forty-four women were on trial on 15 and 16 February for 'breach of the peace' when they danced on the silos at dawn on 1 January 1983. Forty-two of them appeared in court while the other two women decided to go back into the base to show their defiance and contempt for a judicial system obsessed with law and order at the expense of right and wrong.

During the run up to the trial women had discussed whether or not to get experts to give evidence. Some saw it as an opportunity for women who had dedicated their lives to anti-nuclear research, to talk about it publicly, while others preferred to represent themselves. It was hoped that the radio and television would want to interview the experts we called. We decided to invite women only. Some of those charged began their own research and became 'experts' in their own right.

The first day of the trial was mainly filled with the prosecution's case. Our first expert witness gave her evidence at the end of that day. Her subject was Cruise missiles. She explained how they are first strike weapons and are, in fact, no use at all unless used as an offensive. This, of course, makes them prime targets and thus they endanger the very civilians they are purported to protect. Their use is out of British control and these missiles cannot be recalled so an accidental launch could not be corrected. The deployment of Cruise represents a huge escalation in the arms race because the Soviet Union has nothing to compare with them in terms of accuracy and the ability to avoid radar detection. It was pointed out that the British Government has supported the siting of American Cruise in Britain while claiming to be committed to a policy of multilateral disarmament.

The second day of the trial was powerful and upsetting – partly because of the evidence given and partly because of the police's treatment of us. Rosalie Bertell, an American researcher and Catholic nun, gave evidence. She said she'd given up normal life to research into radiation to try and inform people of the real dangers of nuclear proliferation. She said her investigations showed that certain people were particularly susceptible to radiation – those with hereditary diseases like asthma, arthritis, heart disease, allergies etc. These people can be up to 12 times more susceptible to the effects of radiation. This makes a mockery of the so-called 'safe' levels which are worked out with healthy people in mind. People with inherited diseases obviously pass on their low resistance to radiation. Future generations are therefore less able to cope with radiation and yet we are providing them with more and more radioactive material to deal with. Rosalie called this a 'species death process' – we're killing ourselves off. We are the second generation of the atomic age. By the fourth or fifth generation the damage done will be obvious. Whole family lines will have died out by then.

She also talked about research done by Elizabeth Kübler Ross who worked with people approaching death. She drew parallels between a cancer patient and the population at large faced with the prospect of nuclear death. She described the stages of coming to terms with death, as (1) denial, (2) anger, frustration, helplessness, (3) partial acceptance (like cancer patients accepting their condition and taking extra vitamins for it), and (4) the painful reality that becomes your whole life, when you can no longer pretend that things are normal and can no longer ignore the fact that your life is in danger. You take positive action.

Frene Ginwala gave evidence on the conditions of uranium mining in Namibia. Uranium is the raw material from which plutonium for nuclear weapons is made. Nuclear power relies on black people to provide cheap labour. She described how the black workers are dying quickly and regularly, how they have no choice but to do the work. The biggest problem is contamination from uranium which they pass on to their families and friends.

Britain has a direct responsibility for these conditions. Uranium is extracted in Namibia at the Rossing mine, owned by Rio Tinto Zinc, a British multinational. Since Namibia is illegally occupied by South Africa, the taxes on profits made by RTZ and the financing provided by British banks help fund the war South Africa is waging against the national liberation movement SWAPO. The United Nations has declared the extraction, refining and selling of any

Namibian resources illegal for as long as the country remains occupied by South Africa. This ruling has the status of international law, but successive British governments have ignored it and imported Namibian uranium.

Unlike the uranium imported from Australia and Canada which is restricted to civilian use, Namibian uranium has no such restrictions. South Africa has not signed the Non Proliferation Treaty.

At this point more of us gave evidence on things we knew about or had researched. One woman talked about the Genocide Act and the Geneva Convention. Another highlighted the lack of security on the base – if we could get in, so haphazardly and noisily, and then stay on the silos for an hour, it wouldn't be difficult for terrorists to get in. One woman showed Helen Caldicott's video, 'If You Love this Planet', as evidence as to why she'd gone over the fence.

While we were waiting for the verdict a dozen police filed in and stood, arms folded across their chests, between the women in the dock and the supporters. It was deliberate intimidation but we refused to respond. Instead we climbed on to our chairs and reaching over the policemen's heads we held hands with the women on the other side and sang. When the magistrates returned they ordered the police to stand aside.

There was very little about the legal aspects or evidence presented at the trial in the press. They concentrated on the 'carnival atmosphere of political rhetoric' as *The Times* put it. There were no interviews of our experts on television. There was supposed to be a press conference but no press turned up.

The 44 women were found guilty and were bound over to 'keep the peace'. Six women agreed to be bound over – to keep our version of the peace. The other women (except the two who didn't attend the trial) were put in prison for 14 days. *Carole Harwood was one of those women:*

I knew prison would be unpleasant. I'd been arrested at Greenham Common 20 years previously when I was 16. The resulting week in Holloway gaol was no fun. But this time it was different. I was older, perhaps more sensitive, perhaps a little less resilient. I had three children, I knew a little more – at least I thought I did.

After the trial had finished we were taken from the court to waiting vans. The police call them zoo vans; they are in fact riot trucks, consisting of tiny cubicles with wire fronts. There is hardly room to turn round, they are locked individually then double-locked with an iron bolt which runs the full length of the two inward-facing rows. In the event of a crash or a fire . . . nobody said what we were all feeling; for the first time the ten or so women fell silent. We could see the fingers of the women opposite poking through the wire; we were caged, it is an image I still carry with me. The journey to London was long and the driving erratic, but the singing had begun again and the jokes. Slamming his foot on the brakes the driver hurled us backwards and forwards. I'd been sitting down and my head cracked against the metal wall. Asking if everyone was OK, we swapped stories of badly banged kneecaps, shoulders, heads. The policeman sitting at the end of the corridor thought it hugely amusing. No checks were made, no questions asked, my head began to ache. By the following morning I was in a cell with Katrina from the camp, two black women and an older white woman. The headache had become more interesting, producing different images, the windows looked misty, the other women less clear than they should, then there was nothing at all to see and out of that blackness I began to vomit. The older woman had a medical background and looked worried. Katrina rang for a nurse and cradled me. I could hear the other women arguing with the nurse for a doctor. The nurse gave me two disprin and relocked the door. One of the young black women felt the doctor had to be demanded. She was warned by her friends, she would have to make a statement, she could be punished. I wondered what for, Katrina asked what for. The woman's name was Marina. She rang the bell and eventually the doctor came. I was immediately transferred to the hospital wing. I learned later that Marina had been put in solitary for a spell – being on her own was her great fear, as the assistant governor well knew.

Suddenly I was completely isolated, I had no contact with any other Greenham women and I was in a cell on my own. That would teach me! During my time on the wing I learned that it was the only place in the prison where you were expected to scrub on your hands and knees and not use a mop, association was often more limited, exercise sometimes non-existent. I learned that my first impressions had been correct: the hospital wing was also a punishment wing. Sickness is by its nature disruptive, in prisons disruptives are always penalised, there is a logic in it.

Dropping the grill flap the nurse passed me in some sticky, yellow liquid. I asked no questions, I didn't hesitate, me who always reads the small print. I drank it straight down. It was early evening, I didn't wake until the morning. After that I refused all medication. The woman in the cell opposite kept sobbing. She had lost her baby when she was seven months pregnant, it was said as a result of medical incompetence, if not worse, on the part of one of the doctors. The woman in the next cell was very young and had begun having frequent epileptic fits. They took all of the furniture out of her cell (the euphemistic use of 'room' is too offensive), put her mattress on the floor and then locked her in again on her own. The attacks became more and more frequent. She was totally alone, unable to get to the bell when the fits began. She was totally reliant on the women in the adjoining or opposite cells to listen for the telltale noises and ring their bells. This was a sickening realisation for me. From then on I slept with one ear finely tuned. But such fine tuning picks up the unwanted sounds of prisons at night. Regular and endless banging delivered with a monotony of despair, the screams so sharp they started to slice and tear back parts of the mind better left untouched except in nightmares. Sometimes the calls across the night air begging for quiet, for silence, were equally distressing. There could be little chance of silence. This nightly orchestra was being conducted by those in authority, it was the sound of pain and punishment, the consequence of 'crime'. When Angie came round from her fits they pumped her full of valium. Twice a day they bring round drugs. First they ask if anyone needs anything, then does anyone want anything. The alternative to the night music is total oblivion. Play your cards right and you can still feel stoned at lunchtime. Without mass sedation in Britain's prisons there would be riots.

During association and during cleaning I began to make friends with the other prisoners in the hospital wing. One woman had had a hysterectomy only 14 days before. She didn't know if her 15-year-old son was coping on his own. She found carrying the heavy metal buckets full of water a strain. She told me about the guy who'd slipped the drugs into her suitcase and had landed her in Holloway. It was a 57 varieties story I was to hear over and over again in different forms. Her man had got her to carry drugs (both with and without her knowledge) and then pretended he had nothing to do with it. A boyfriend had put her on the game and after all it was her risk, not his, and he did visit sometimes. Abandoned wives making ends meet with shoplifting, their man's interest and

108

financial commitment ceasing the moment they walked out through the door.

It was with horror I watched the pattern emerge. As a feminist I knew women were oppressed by men. As a feminist I knew nothing. I had gone to prison with the arrogant notion that we 36 Greenham women were political prisoners. After a few days I realised all 300 of us were political prisoners and that the common link had a gender, it was male.

Politically it was a relief. Personally it was agony.

Gradually a new perspective on my own particular experiences since I'd arrived in Holloway, formed. Why I was there, who'd put me there. On arrival we had to remove our clothes for a male doctor. What was his motivation, what job satisfaction is there for a male doctor in a women's prison? There certainly wasn't much evidence of compassion, and lots of real fear and hostility from the women. The links seemed more obvious still.

Even within a female prison men have positions of power. You may wish to see an assistant governor about something intensely personal and find yourself face to face with a man. While I was on the hospital wing my mother rang the guy in charge of my wing and he was utterly charming. He assured and reassured her. There was no Carole Harwood on the hospital wing, she was quite well, was receiving the special diet her doctor had written about and there was absolutely no cause for worry. He would come and give me messages from my mother implying she was glad I was recovering. He was lying through his teeth and I have a letter of apology written by the prison authorities some weeks after my release to prove it!

Yet it was a shock. I expected the people in charge to play fair and they turned out to be the real crooks in Holloway. I learned how a letter from one famous inmate had been intercepted and sold to the *Sun*. I learned that if you refused 'reasonable orders', male warders could be brought in, that they could strip search and 'restrain' you. I learned something about the corruption and oppression that was prison life and I found it unendurable. It felt like institutional rape.

Being separated from my friends and being always alone accentuated the panic I felt rising and the anger and the dull ache of knowing things would never be the same. That a whole area of my life I was (mostly) comfortable with would have to change. I'd always hoped to slip into a serene middle age, a bit of peace and quiet. This was going to screw it all up. I felt sick with fear.

109

Although I'd been passed as fit to return to the ordinary prison the day after I'd been hospitalised, my repeated requests to go back with my friends were refused, hedged and refused again. I began to be resigned to spending the whole 14 days alone, when the story broke in the *Guardian* and I was moved back the same day. I was so overjoyed to see the other Greenham women, yet could sense my own reserve. I felt changed and disordered.

But it was good and fun. The atmosphere lighter and happier. I became close friends with a black mother of three, we swapped stories: babies, labour, operations. She made me laugh till the tears streamed down my face and they tasted different to the ones I'd been having. She told me how she'd stack her freezer with the most exotic foods in the supermarket, how her kids complained they didn't like asparagus so why did she steal it, why not beans. She explained to them that then they could choose, they could turn down asparagus if they wanted. She had brought the four of them up single-handed and had managed to give them that choice.

On the last night when we realised the other prisoners had planned a sort of farewell party – singing songs about what we were doing and how it was for them too – we cried because we were moved but also because we felt that we were walking out on them. What's 14 days after all?

The giving of a last scrap of face cream to you, a stranger, because you look like you need it. And the flowers. I wouldn't have believed flowers could have made such a difference. Especially when I was on my own I rearranged them every day, slept with them at my bedside, smelled and kissed them. A woman I didn't know sent me in a tiny bunch of snowdrops. She will never know how precious they were to me.

Six months have now passed and it has been every bit as difficult as I'd feared. On the anniversary of the founding of the camp I was asked on the radio about the unacceptable lifestyle at Greenham and the interviewer quoted from that morning's *Daily Mail*. After all it was a peak listening show and he'd managed to get hold of a respectable face of protest woman, married with three children. It was going out live and I was to be the reassurance. 'And we all know about the charges (!) of lesbianism at the peace camp.'

I knew what he wanted and expected me to say. My mouth went all dry and the palms of my hands all wet. He smiled encouragingly. I told him if the thought of women making love with one another was more threatening than the idea of men making war with each other, then I found that frightening. I said a bit more, making the connections between male violence and war, talking about the media treatment of rape, pornography, Greenham women. The friendly breakfast show personality went paler and I swear his eyes narrowed, just like in the stories. He didn't say goodbye as I left the studio, nor politely stand as he'd done when I arrived. Sometimes I think all the old virtues are disappearing.


While these women were in prison a vigil had been set up outside the entrance to Holloway. Gradually stories of women held on remand for months at a time for petty crimes, and of the way some women were treated by warders, began filtering out with the visitors. We were beginning to learn the real function of prisons – to remind us of our lowly place in the pecking order of power and punish those who challenge that power, out of need or conscience. We learned too about the petty power games and institutionalised violence perpetrated under the guise of 'justice'.

In an attempt to draw attention to the plight of women prisoners, six women decided to take action. In the early hours of February 25 they climbed *into* Holloway and up on to the roof.

Some weeks later they appeared in court to answer charges of 'inciting prisoners to riot'. Before the case was heard a mock trial was held outside the courthouse. Holloway was charged with inhumane treatement and was found guilty.

*Fiona Campbell, one of the six women, describes what happened during their trial*: One of the longer term prisoners came as a witness. The prosecution asked her whether the noise level was different that morning and she answered 'Yes, it was quieter.' she went on to explain that this was because everybody was glued to their radios listening to what was going on.

We were all represented by Jane Hickman, except for me. I represented myself so that I could ask questions of the warders that lawyers would not be permitted to ask. Questions about the woman who had set herself on fire three years earlier in Holloway: her cries for help were ignored and she burned to death. Questions about food, conditions and the fact that once the cells are locked up at night, the warders don't get keys for the cells until the morning. It was revealed that if women continually make noises to get attention, they're put into the punishment cell and the hospital wing.

When both sides of the case had been presented the magistrate retired to consider the evidence. The verdict was 'Not Guilty'.

Back in October 1982, 21 women had decided to transfer their voting address to the camp.

*Aggie Jakubska is a sculptor who moved to Greenham from Dorset:* For me this was an important thing. Greenham was my home and I wanted to transfer my vote. I didn't want to waste it.

In the week after 12 December some of us went to the court hearing that was going on to decide this, so that we'd be able to present our answers to objections that had been raised. The case was heard by a Registrar of Electors in Council Chamber at Newbury District Council House, this horrible room without any windows and a weird strip light that makes your eyes vibrate. The chief objection was that we weren't legal residents because we didn't have a residence, a house with four walls, a roof, windows, garden etc. – a home, as they put it. I hadn't really put my case together, but when I realised how they were going to put it to the court, using the word 'home', it suddenly started meaning something to me.

In the lunch recess I rushed over to Barbara's to look up 'home' in the Oxford English Dictionary. Nowhere, in all the definitions, did it mention anything about there being a structure where 'home' is concerned; it was much more to do with feelings and associations with a particular place. The home consisted of people rather than a house, and what you felt towards those people.

Well I staggered in to court with this whacking great dictionary under my arm and we all had a turn to sit in the witness box to answer questions and put our case. How long had we been there? What was our home? Each woman sat there and described her bender or tent, what it was made of and how long she'd been living in it, what she felt about the place and why she was there. We each said different sorts of things. Then I got up, plonked the OED on the desk and said I wanted to read from this book some definitions of the word 'home' which I completely agreed with because they explained in a more succinct way how I was feeling about it. How could anyone dispute the linguistic Bible of the English Language! Even though I sleep mainly in my car, which I also use as a vehicle, it is not my home. I live in this place because I wish to be with the

112

women I love, trust and share objectives with, and even though I've lived in many places before, here, for the first time in my life, I feel at home. I said that when our joint aim of getting rid of the missiles and the base is achieved, I would like to continue to live in this part of the world because I found it beautiful – except the part of the common covered by the base.

I could see that the Registrar was listening and that what I was saying was going in. A fortnight later we were notified that the objections to our being on the electoral register had been dismissed.

It was finally acknowledged that Greenham was our home, but legal proceedings were still under way to get us permanently removed from the site.

In early February 1983 the NDC secured High Court injunction writs on the 21 women named on the electoral register. On 27 January, in a private meeting of a few select councillors, the common land byelaws were revoked, thereby giving the NDC private landlord rights. As private landlords they were then able, within the law, to apply for injunctions against named trespassers.

The writ was composed of two charges. The first was 'Conspiracy to trespass'. If this charge was proven, it would mean that the 21 women would be banned from the common for life. It went further. If any of these women issued an explicit invitation to another person to trespass and that person agreed, then they could be imprisoned for up to two years.

The second charge was 'Conspiracy to incite others to trespass'. If this was proven, it would mean two years' imprisonment for even mentioning Greenham Common or Cruise missiles.

We were summoned to appear at the High Court in London on 9 March. The support for the trial was overwhelming, the floor of the hall outside a sea of women, listening as judges would never listen, to women's words in defence of their home. Inside the court men play-acted justice.

By late afternoon it was over. Injunctions were secured for the first charge, but not for the second. All 21 women were banned for life from setting foot over the imaginary lines that define 'Greenham Common'.

# 14
# Talking Through Our Trips
# to Other Places

The women's web grows, the network spreads. All the time new connections are being made with individuals and groups of women, here and abroad. Greenham women have gone on trips all over the world meeting others, talking about Greenham, taking part in conferences, demonstrations and direct actions. We have been joining up the dots on the map and seeing the stranglehold the military has over people in this and every country.

We feel it essential to increase our understanding of the role of the British military. Ireland seems the obvious place to begin. We can compare what we saw there with our own experience of British troops at home and the American military occupation of our country through its 102 bases here. We also feel that we have a responsibility to understand the Irish question. We set out to learn.[1]

*Gerry Ellis is a despatch rider living in a housing co-op in London. She was one of the six Greenham women who went to Belfast in Northern Ireland. They joined a picket outside Armagh women's jail to mark International Women's Day, 8 March 1983:*
Although some of us felt reluctant to enter 'the troubles', the grim pattern of random deaths, bombings and shootings which have characterised the state of Northern Ireland since its inception, we also felt a preference for first-hand information.

By visiting Belfast we were able to get a glimpse of what goes on behind the news and even those two days provided an unforgettable insight into the way the media selection of events manufactures public opinion. In Britain, all television coverage has to be carefully vetted by the IBA, and editors of leading newspapers are wary of anything 'controversial' which may be 'offensive to public decency'. As a result, typical press coverage amounts to little more than a body count. The issues are treated as non-existent and British

114

involvement is never questioned, but taken for granted. Officially British troops are a neutral peace-keeping force, while in reality there are thousands of unpublicised accounts of situations where they provoke violence and pursue a campaign of sectarian harassment.

One of the concealed issues is the struggle Irish prisoners have maintained for political status. Due to the official distinction between keeping the peace and fighting a war, deaths resulting from British bullets are legitimised within the context of official army activities, whilst armed retaliation from paramilitary groups is tried and sentenced in criminal courts as murder. In May 1980, when nine IRA prisoners went on hunger strike for political recognition, first one, Bobby Sands, also an elected MP to Westminster, died, then ten more, leaving a legend behind them.

The picket was a way of linking the women in Armagh jail with other female political prisoners throughout the world.

Our approach to Belfast was accompanied by increased clampdown and surveillance. Ten minutes from the station our car was stopped by a road block. Two young soldiers, one white, one black, with camouflage jackets and rifles, opened up the back of the car and rummaged through the bags although they didn't check the contents. It was more of a routine harassment than a search for anything specific. Drivers are made to show their photographed licences as proof of identity.

At the community centre, a photographic exhibition included an account of the campaign for abortion and contraception rights. One thing that both the Protestant and the Catholic church have in common is a determination to withhold these rights from women.

Some Belfast women described the campaign they were mounting for decent housing. They eventually got their complaints heard by picketing the housing offices and yelling all day to the relevant officials through loud-hailers. The Sinn Fein is also organising housing committees in response to conditions which are some of the worst in Europe. A large percentage of houses lack basic amenities like kitchens and bathrooms. Overcrowding is worst in Catholic parts of the city, while houses remain vacant in Protestant areas due to sectarian harassment. The rates of social security and unemployment benefit are lower than in Britain on the grounds that prices are lower, although food, electricity and other basics actually cost more.

Although many millions of British taxpayers' money is poured

115

into Northern Ireland each year, most of it is spent on courts, prisons and police rather than being used to alleviate social conditions. New housing estates are being designed, but to military specifications, in order to aid surveillance.

Visually the environment tells the same story of a vicious circle of poverty, rebellion, repression. Sometimes an entire terrace of houses is bricked up. What was a street is now a solid wall, with new bricks where there used to be doors and windows. Concrete ramps are laid across the roads at regular intervals. They are known as dead policemen and are another measure to inhibit sniper attacks, by slowing down traffic. Black taxis operate a kind of bus service along the city's main routes. The bus service was withdrawn because buses were too easily converted into road blocks. Taxis collect passengers from bus stops, you pay the driver as you get out and it's rarely more than 30p.

Social security offices and police stations are encased in fine wire cages around and above, laced with barbed wire, with cameras mounted at street corners. The police stations are guarded by a sentry box, a watching eye and rifle butt peeping through the narrow slit. Women sometimes have threatening comments made at them from the men inside.

By contrast, vivid wall paintings strike back at the urban decay, picturing images of revolution, names and faces become legendary, portraits, poems, slogans, some expressed solidarity with the Palestine Liberation Organisation. A popular symbol is of a flying dove, carrying a gun in its feet. It is dubbed the spirit of freedom. A reminder that the non-violent civil rights movement died on the streets on Bloody Sunday, 30 January 1972, when British troops opened fire on unarmed civil demonstrators.

The Armagh picket was organised by the London–Armagh Co-ordinating Committee and the women's department of the Sinn Fein, backed up by the people of Belfast who provided cars and drivers, let us stay in their homes, and arranged entertainment both evenings.

Four coaches left the Falls Road about noon on Sunday. We were intercepted about halfway to Armagh jail by the Royal Ulster Constabulary. Two of them, guns in hand, made their way up the centre of the coach, unrolling and studying posters of the event, sifting bags in the luggage rack, and making random searches of handbags. There were about 250 women and 15 men on the picket (both English and Irish), and a third as many RUC police. Their

116

presence had a considerably more threatening aspect than the throngs of boys in blue which surround Greenham actions. The RUC are a paramilitary police force, they all wore bullet-proof vests, carried guns, and drove heavily shielded landrovers.

Armagh jail has been picketed annually on International Women's Day for several years. In previous years police road blocks prevented the picket from gathering directly outside the jail, so that prisoners only heard about it indirectly, but this year we were allowed right up to the perimeter wall. Messages of support were read out and also delivered to the prisoners inside. The name of each prisoner was read out to a chorus of 'We support you'. A cheer went up as a dress was thrown out of a window in response. It was the only and unexpected signal that women inside were able to hear the demonstration.

After the picket, the coaches took everybody back to the Falls Road where 50 of us squeezed into the women's centre for a discussion. For many this was our first opportunity to express our shock and disbelief at what we had seen. The group contained a variety of different political affiliations and differing levels of political involvement, and all kinds of issues and questions were raised. There was some discussion about how relevant Greenham-type tactics of non-violence were to the kind of political struggle the Irish women were confronting, but it was too big a question to resolve there and then. We moved on to look at the connections between what was happening in Northern Ireland and its implications for mainland Britain.

It was pointed out that the British armed forces, highly trained and on active service in Ireland, were not kept in readiness just for international conflicts, but also to counter civil unrest. Plastic bullets have been used for several years in Northern Ireland against civilians. Protest against their use is only now gaining ground in Britain because they are being stockpiled by the police force in mainland Britain.[2] We were reminded that our present Head of Police, Kenneth Newman, served his apprenticeship in Northern Ireland, and since his appointment the new Police Bill has been introduced, containing measures already common practice there.

It's a common belief in England that being in blatant contravention of the international code of human rights is something other countries do. Dictatorships do that sort of thing, not democracies, and it is to prevent the spread of it that a nuclear deterrent is needed. The hypocrisy underlying this kind of mythology is well

117

illustrated by the experiences of the women in Armagh jail. They are not given the rights of ordinary suspects, such as trial by jury, yet they are denied the status of political prisoners. Strip searches are now common practice even though the prisoner is accompanied at all times by a warden. Prisoners who refuse have been denied visitors and hospital treatment. Otherwise they may be carried out by force by several male wardens, who may also blindfold and beat the women. This ritual degradation of women is even carried to the lengths of making them wash male prisoners' underpants. Visitors smuggle out this information at the risk of having their visits stopped.

What we saw was the tail end of a process that has been going on since the twelfth century. The toll in human lives runs into hundreds of thousands. Many children are on valium. The psychological damage resulting from violence which has become an integral part of daily life is incalculable. But the side-effects don't end there. People who have learnt to live by the gun now know no other profession. Wife-battering is more frequent than in either the rest of Britain or Ireland. Where households include members of para-military organisations, guns are also used to intimidate wives. Since 1969, active service in Northern Ireland has made the British Army able to boast of being one of the best trained in the world. The six counties are now a kind of social laboratory for the legal and investigative measures equivalent to a police state.

Back in London I felt I had to reassess non-violence. Had I been born in Belfast I too might have opposed British imperialism and ended up in Armagh jail. It seemed to me the value of non-violence is that it may be the only form of protest which will not provoke a totalitarian response – the only way to gain freedom without losing it in the process. It avoids the conditions where violence breeds violence and erodes human dignity.

Although non-violence has been tried and has failed in Northern Ireland, I still wanted to understand why. Non-violent direct action works by being able to mobilise massive public support against a recognised injustice. However its success depends on the free flow of information. If courts and media can be leaned on to misrepresent the facts, they indirectly provoke the escalation of violence. This, in turn, plays directly into the hands of those who wish to introduce totalitarian methods of control.

I can't provide a hopeful conclusion here. I can only conclude that if non-violence is to work, we have to reclaim the values of

118

justice and free speech and make them meaningful again.

By connecting examples, we build up a picture of male violence all over the world. Here we are threading together the repressive regime in Ireland with the brutal macho behaviour of police in Sicily – Sicily again a victim of invasion, another USAF outpost for American Cruise missiles, another fortress island like Britain.

*Aggie Jakubska:* Living at Greenham for nine months had been a political and emotional crash course and an intensive self-questioning and re-learning time for me. A time of rejection of old, ingrained behaviour patterns, a period of gestation enabling me to build confidence in my new self. I hadn't realised what a frightening and intense experience it would be when I decided to go to Sicily for International Women's Day to join seven other women from Greenham and hundreds of women from many different countries, in actions against the siting of Cruise missiles there. I went because I had become very aware of the multinational nature of the nuclear war machine and my need to de-nationalise my own ideas about protesting against it. I cannot see the American Cruise missile issue as a parochial one, local only to the country that is crazy enough to accept them. Nuclear radiation would not respect national boundaries, it cannot be localised, all Europe and beyond would cop it – if the superpowers decided to play out their power game in the European 'Theatre of War'. The consequences of siting Cruise in Sicily scare me just as much, if not more, than they do at Greenham. There on the southernmost edge of Europe, they can be threateningly pointed at the Middle East, a region right now in an explosive warring state. Some of these countries already have nuclear capability; all they require is a good excuse, as a defensive tactic of course, to use it. Libya has openly threatened retaliation if the missiles are brought to Sicily.

In the main square of the small Sicilian town of Comiso, near Magliocco air base, the projected site of 112 American Cruise missiles, sits the statue of Diana, the Virgin Goddess. She is Virgin, meaning unpossessed and undominated by men, her own woman, strong, wilful. The Piazza Fonte Diana is where the men of the town meet each evening to gossip, make deals, and discuss how they are running the world. She sits and listens to them, biding her time, calling quietly to us. We answered her call. During that week hundreds of women came together in Comiso and the nearby Magliocco air base to reclaim these places from the Patriarchs – to protest against male violence in all its forms, from the rape of individual women to the rape of our planet.

On Sunday, 6 March women had gathered in the piazza named for Diana, and hitherto the preserve of the men (it is lined with bars and banks, concrete symbols of materialism and male control). The women grouped in the middle of the piazza and formed a circle which grew outwards, expanding more and more, pushing the astonished men out of the space. This was a supportive demonstration for Gina, a 17-year-old Comiso girl who had been raped at gunpoint by three men a couple of months before, and who had had the courage to defy social convention and denounce her attackers. Since then she had been imprisoned at home by her parents.

On 8 March the focus was Magliocco air base. A 50-strong international group of women with Italian and local Sicilian women made a sit-down protest outside the main gates of the base. We sat in a circle and wove a huge multicoloured web by throwing balls of wool between us. We sang, and learned each other's songs in our different languages. We shared our power and strengthened our emotional bonds. There was little traffic using the main gate that day and we were not blocking access, yet while we were there a contingent of police arrived, equal in number to us, and surrounded our circle. They stood about, first variously bemused then openly sneering, eyeing our bodies, passing remarks about us. After a while our circle stood up, the web raised above our heads we moved together towards the gates of the base. Carabinieri scurried to shut them and form a defensive barrier in front. As we approached and surged around them, the men became entangled in the multi-coloured strands. At first they treated it all as a joke, but quickly their grins hardened, reverted to grimaces of fear as they flailed about desperately trying to rip themselves free of wool and the close contact with the women. They struggled more and more violently, and at last tore the body of the web away from themselves and us and threw it triumphantly into a large puddle by the side of the road. They laughed weakly and we watched sadly as one of us waded in and pulled it from the muddy water, like a net of rainbow fish. Some policemen approached the sodden mass, lying there, poked at it disgustedly and quickly withdrew their feet as if they might be contaminated. It was like an afterbirth. It appeared to be dead. They seemed to have won.

That evening we walked back to the town to join in a huge march of 600 women through the streets of Comiso, which had been organised by the 'Coordinamento della Donne', a women's group from Catania in Sicily. It was a demo Italian style – very noisy, slogans stridently shouted through loudhailers and lots of placards bearing strong statements, protesting against male violence in all its aspects.

The next morning women converged again at the main gate of the missile base. This time with the intention of preventing workers and lorry traffic from passing. Around 40 of us sat down, arms linked across the gateway. Police immediately shut it to prevent us from entering and re-directed the traffic, and then proceeded to break up the blockade by roughly pulling women apart and dragging them away. At no point did any of us use verbal abuse or physical incitement against the police – just our being there was enough to elicit an aggressive reaction from them. Women who were clinging to the metal lattice of the gates were abused, had their hands kicked at, their fingers twisted by police on the inside. Those outside dragged us, pushed us so violently that a Swiss woman's arm was broken. During all this the media was conspicuous by its absence. Photographers who witnessed police violence were apprehended. I was roughed up by three policemen and had the evidence confiscated; my camera broken open and the film ripped out. We decided to end the blockade before there were any more injuries. Plainclothes police who had been standing by watching, demanded to see every woman's identity card or passport and noted down all the details.

It took us a day to recover from the shock of the brutality and ferocity of the police reaction to our non-violence. By Friday, 11 March, most of our number had dispersed and gone back home. During that night a group of women who were walking around the perimeter fence of the base, were followed by a jeep, shots were heard and they were accosted by soldiers who shouted obscenities and jabbed at them with bayonetted guns.

Early the next morning, at 6.30 a.m., a dozen women sat down across the road leading to the main gates of the base. A queue of workers' vehicles soon built up but some of the cars turned and drove way. Police marched down from the gates and proceeded to drag us to the side of the road and beckoned traffic to pass, then they retreated and we sat down in the road again. The traffic queue built up – the police descended on us and pulled women by their hair, dragged us by a wrist or ankle, twisting it at the same time, to inflict as much pain as possible. Women were deliberately dragged to and fro through mud and thrown violently on top of each other and held down with policemen's feet while the traffic went by. This procedure was repeated six times. Each time the police brutality increased, as did their obvious enjoyment of it. I was disgusted to realise that they were getting off on it.

That did it for me. I couldn't bear to let myself be touched by them again. Sitting down once more would mean them touching, dragging me – loving it. I decided to get up and do something else useful. As inconspicuously as possible I got into our van which was parked nearby, in order to try to get photographs of what was happening. I was shit scared after what happened two days before. If I was noticed they would rip open the van and haul me out. Just then, after an hour of repeated blockading, a high-ranking police officer's car drew up by the women sitting in the road and the officer advised them that they were being arrested. One woman who decided to walk away was dragged back and placed in a police van, as was a woman who was acting as legal observer. Just as the police van drove off towards Comiso, a conspicuously large, official-looking car with American number plates drove quickly by and into the base. The 12 women, after spending two hours cooped up in the van outside the police station at Comiso, were taken to the prison in nearby Ragusa.

That evening women gathered again in the Piazza Fonte Diana for a candlelit vigil. Slowly and quietly in a dignified manner we walked around the square carrying candles, wearing on our backs placards telling of the day's events. Then we stood in a silent circle while the men behind us read and commented in hushed tones. The unusual silence of the demonstration clearly affected those watching, as it reflected our feelings of stunned sadness and outrage at the brutality of the police towards our women and the destruction of the international peace camp which the police had evicted and burnt down that afternoon. The light of the candles in the twilight expressed our determination to overcome the terrible violence surrounding us, but by a different means. By the power of women's spirit, and in a non-violent way. We placed 12 candles on the ground in the shape of a woman's sign and sent our love and our strength to the women in prison.

The provincial prison, the 'Carcere Ragusa', is an intimidating medieval fortress-like structure. Its massive bullet-pockmarked walls are floodlit orange at night, guards with guns patrol the battlements. The group which came to Comiso from Greenham had been eight women. It was so painful to be separated by those massive walls from four of our friends and from our new friends from different countries: wondering what sort of treatment they were getting, knowing only that we could not visit them because just parents or relations were allowed. One day, when we were singing outside the walls to communicate that we were there, the women inside sang back the news that Skeeter's arm had been broken during the blockade on Friday and that she had, after many demands, been taken to hospital. We, outside, spent five frustrating days with constantly changing information as to the legal position of the imprisoned women.

*One of those arrested, Peggy, a Dutch woman, kept a diary:*
*Saturday, 12 March, the second day in prison.* At last, I've got some paper and a pen. What are they going to do with us? The uncertainty about this is becoming disturbing. Yesterday it looked as if they would release us today, but now it's getting clear to me that we will be locked up here till at least Tuesday. Again I experience how awful men are and how nice women. After the police station yesterday the prison was nearly a relief.

Who would have thought that I should have to try to catch sunbeams through bars? I would like to know if the news of our imprisonment has already reached Holland; does Claudia already know and my family and all the others? What do they think and what are they going to do with it?

I'm so glad that I'm not in a cell on my own but together with Bee. It's great how every time any of us meet on the corridor, we embrace each other and exchange the latest information.

When you ask Them what's going to happen, they say that blockading a road is liable to a punishment of one to five years and if you did it with a group (like we did) it's even twice as long. I have to be careful not to start puzzling about this because I think I don't have to take this too seriously because of the international character of our group. I feel quite strong and also very conscious of the fact that it was good what we did and that it is their system which is ridiculous! I realise the good sides of being in prison: all the publicity now already in Italy and when they keep us here longer a lot of international publicity as well.

*Monday, 14 March, fourth day in prison.* Yesterday I became more and more down. The worst is that with everything we ask they keep us on a string. Telegrams? Domani! Phone calls? Domani! Visitors? Domani! Our stuff (we don't even have toothbrushes)? Domani! In the afternoon there was a shouting action of women in front of the prison to get us free. That felt so great. I nearly had to cry hearing the other women's voices. We've been singing (we weren't allowed to shout back) that Skeeter is in hospital but I wonder if they've got that message because there didn't come a reaction.

They play with our dependency, they provoke us, the bastards. That is maybe what drives us mad most here, in this wing of the prison. The female warders are very kind to us which is confusing because when you want to protest, for example by making a lot of noise, it affects them directly instead of the prison authorities. Besides that, we're also scared to protest because you constantly feel that they've the power to do everything they want with you, isolate you, or worse. Anna-Luisa told me that one of the guards had said, 'Why do you sing? Don't you realise you are in prison? We can even kill you.'

What really keeps me going are the serious talks about setting up a women's peace camp this summer in Comiso – if they don't forbid us to go back to Italy. I hope they don't do this to us. That would be a disaster!

*Aggie*: On Tuesday night we heard that there was a chance the women might be released the next day on certain conditions, rather like a 'bind over' to keep the peace. It was hard to trust this after hearing so many contradictory statements during the past few days, even though we saw 12 exit papers with their names on. Believing would be seeing them walk out of prison.

Eventually two police vans appeared. The group of supporters was pushed out and the vans reversed into the hallway of the prison. Then, suddenly we saw them, beaming and calling our names as they were hustled into the vans and quickly driven off. There was just an instant to touch and kiss the woman who was by an open window as the van swept by, heading, we learned, for the main police station. The women had been granted provisional liberty by the interrogating judge – only to be handed straight over into police custody!

Outside the gates of the police station, women linked arms in a circle and we sang, 'You can't kill the spirit, she is like a mountain, old and strong she goes on and on'. It is a chant that raises energy at times when you may feel you have little left. Suddenly we could hear shouting and singing from the windows above us. A hand waved and then we heard shutters slamming inside. One very agile woman climbed up the parapet and exchanged frantic greetings before being shut off. We demanded that the women be allowed to receive some of their belongings, in person, before being expelled. Amazingly enough, each one was let out individually for half a minute's excited conversation through the iron gates. The women looked radiant, full of power, and this gave us renewed strength. Their power seemed to be multiplied as a result of their ordeal, as well as by all the energy we had concentrated and directed towards them. You could feel it swirling around us – they had just refused to sign the agreement for their expulsion.

Then at around 10 in the evening a convoy of police vans left for Palermo airport. The women were taken, with a heavy and armed police escort, to Rome where they were put on a plane for London. The Dutch, German and Danish women were flown or put on a train directly to their own countries. The one Italian woman was freed.

Although we had issued daily press releases detailing the happenings in Comiso, stressing the peaceful nature of our actions as opposed to the ferocious over-reaction of the police and the Italian Government who seemed to think they were dealing with violent terrorists, the response of the British press was minimal. The attitude of some journalists parochial. The news was not spectacular enough. One said that a woman's death would have created more interest. The Italian press coverage was fuller, but played down the fact that it was a non-violent women's action, avoided descriptions of police brutality and minimised the action's obvious effectiveness. After the expulsion was ordered the main political parties issued a statement supporting the government's effort in maintaining 'law and order' and saying that: 'The siting of Cruise missiles at Comiso could not be prevented by initiative of doubtful democratic credibility', forgetting to notice the unconstitutional behaviour of the Minister of the Interior in expelling the women without just cause and without a trial or sentence.

Even before the blockades and arrest, the idea had been floating among us of linking up all the energy women had brought to Comiso, not just for the occasion of International Women's Day, but more permanently. In this macho place we recognised a desperate need and felt the urgency for a women's non-violent initiative to continue. The confusion and the party-political bias of the men who ran the existing peace camp reinforced this need.

In April 1983 our association of women from all over Europe bought a piece of farm land right next to the Magliocco base on which to site our camp. From the ashes of the mixed peace camp burnt down by the police, the Women's International Peace Camp 'La Ragnatela' – 'The Spiderweb' – was born.


Like Britain, Italy is an occupied country, whose government is coerced by the United States into repressing its own people. We move now to the US Government's repression within its own national boundaries. Three women from Greenham went on a speaking tour through America. *One of them, Theresa McGinley, had been living on a farm in Scotland before she moved to Greenham in late 1982. She describes her experience in America: All the Way to America?* – When I heard about the tour in America I had a picture in my mind of women being used as superstars then of women being exploited, pushed and guilt-tripped into working in a way that clearly contradicts the work we do here at the camp. Other women's experience of touring had worried me. One example that sticks very vividly in my mind, was when Anna and Babs toured Denmark. They were put on stages with military generals who used such things as slide shows and video equipment to reinforce their views on the arms race, whilst Anna and Babs didn't even have an adequate interpreter. It seemed crazy to me that we could continue to fall into the same traps where lessons had already been painfully learnt.

The demand for women from Greenham to go out and talk has escalated so fast and reached a peak with this proposed trip to America. There was pressure on us to respond quickly as the tour had already been organised. Three women had said they would do it. For many of us, outreach is a crucial part of our work. But serious questioning of the style, content, and the demands and expectations of our hosts had to be worked through. The invitation came at a time when many influences were working to uproot and divert our energy and spirit. There was a need in myself, and other women, to work from a base where we could be in touch with ourselves and with each other, and where we were coming from. I believed this tour was necessary for communications and became aware of how powerful it could be, but also of its potential to

126

damage if women were rendered powerless in front of others with high expectations of them . . . or if women played along with the role of celebrity or got into power trips. Women who are travelling across the globe because of their involvement with Greenham carry with them a huge responsibility because of representation and influence. I needed to trust the women who would be going.

Then suddenly more changes (the only thing I recognise as consistent around here!). Jean, who was going, dropped out. I had a lot going through my head about the tour. I talked with Caroline, Toni and London Theresa about it and then made a decision to go. I spoke with many women at the camp. I didn't want to step on anyone, and the response I got was very inspiring for me. I felt trusted, even encouraged, to go ahead with my decision.

I don't feel I can give any detailed account of what the tour involved. I can only pass on my reflections. The question I obviously have to ask myself is 'Was it all worth it?' There were many obvious and underground influences working to disrupt the tour, their expectations of us were more powerful than I expected, and I had to put so much energy into hanging on to my very core, my sanity; the basics.

The whirlwind of enthusiasm we entered had hurricane potential. The women who organised the tour, had set up contacts with a whole network of people on the east, west, north and south, and a bit in the middle. 'Do you want these Greenham women in your area?' It seemed no one had said 'No'. They wanted so much from us. Communication between where we had come from and where we went seemed non-existent so wherever we happened to be, they wanted as much mileage out of us as possible. We were also very useful. Through us, a voice could be given to the very valuable work these people were doing in their own areas.

One day's agenda, beginning at eight in the morning, consisted of four separate press interviews, four radio interviews, a public meeting plus a formal dinner on top of all the travelling. I knew why I was there. But what does it mean to struggle for freedom, then to go out and work in a way that contradicts what I believe in? Therefore what was the sense in allowing myself to be swallowed up? Why should I fulfil all the demands, play into the hands of established assumptions, celebrity approval and the traditional roles of public speaking? I find it intimidating to stand before people and project my views in these unnatural circumstances. So, for the three of us, a continual breaking down of these barriers was essential, almost never using a stage or microphone, trying always to rearrange seats into circles and opening up the meetings to discussion where we could share with people on an equal basis.

We had to keep asking why the reporters couldn't come together for one big meeting or, better still, why don't they come to our meetings? It wasn't very often that changes could be made because of the pressure put on us, and the three of us had different ideas about what was exploitation and what was necessary work.

We were pressed for autobiographies from which a leaflet could be produced, a form of presentation I couldn't be a part of. I was pressed also to use my surname. I didn't want to. I suppose I felt this is one part of me you ain't getting. I didn't find it relevant, and I could see how easily I could be made a spokesperson or, worse still, a spokesman!

The response we were getting from the people was overwhelming. It was inspiring to meet so many involved in work against twentieth-century insanity. I got a strong sense of solidarity and support that deepened my conviction for my work. Sometimes though, it was too much. A standing ovation before we even opened our mouths left me feeling the message to share didn't carry the importance I wanted it to. Occasionally I felt if we had sat there and picked our noses, the response would have been the same.

The tour lasted six weeks. In that time we covered 31 different cities, some smaller towns, plus infiltrating into suburbia. We had two unscheduled days which I looked forward to as a chance to recharge myself. But nae, 'twas only enough to stop me from dying. The three of us slept for two days solid and were left with a greater sense of not being able to continue. We were in the midst of a crisis. Caroline and I had even arranged our own kidnappings with a wonderful woman we had met. Eventually we sorted it out by calling an emergency meeting, and with the help of another woman who helped organise the tour, were able to dissolve the intensity of the next two weeks. There were times when all I wanted to do was end the tour. But a lot of effort and money had gone into it, and sometimes I felt trapped.

Whilst in America I gained a stronger sense of what's against us. Anyone working against established values, against the state, against the stranglehold of patriarchal authority, is taking an enormous risk. The illusion of the American dream must be kept flying high, free from contamination of a communist influence at all costs.

128

I spoke with many people involved in work advocating human life, dignity and rights. It was terrifying to hear of confrontations they came across from the Government's underground spy networks – CIA or FBI? All movements are infiltrated by agents. Some sections of the anti-nuclear peace movement are sponsored entirely by government, advocating anti-ballistic missiles as our only salvation. Our tour was being attacked and disrupted by these networks. My experience at immigration was a good example. I was taken aside for no apparent reason, the entire contents of my bag were tipped out, my diaries and personal letters read, I was repeatedly asked what organisation I worked for, checked out on computers and had my photograph taken. From there a whole series of incidents which, on their own, could have been coincidences, collectively created quite a frightening picture. A woman's car parked outside one of our meetings was smashed up. After another meeting we were driven to a bar where the woman driver had her keys stolen from her jacket pocket. The car was found two blocks away and the only thing missing was our case which contained the photography exhibition on Greenham Common Women. The exhibition was incredible. It managed to tell a complete herstory of its own. Also taken were our leaflets, diaries, journals, hmmm . . . Aeroplane reservations were mysteriously cancelled and from then on we booked seats in pseudonyms. Press conferences were blacked out. A woman organising one sent out 30 invitations in good time for postal delays, but not one of them was received before or after the conference.

Caroline and myself arrived at 6.30 one morning in Georgia, South Carolina, expecting to be picked up by two women. As soon as we stepped off the train a taxi driver rushed up to us. 'Your friends can't make it. They've asked me to drive you there.' I asked, 'How far to Athens?' 'Forty miles,' he said. 'It will take an hour to get there.' Unsuspecting and half asleep we got in. An hour later we arrived in the middle of a forest forty miles in the opposite direction. We insisted he drive us back to the station. He mumbled, 'I've picked up the wrong people.' On our return to the station Caroline took our phone contact numbers out of her pocket and he snatched them out of our hands. We made a huge scene and got them back. Thirty dollars he wanted for the journey but he didn't fuss when we said we had no money – off he ran.

Meanwhile panic had set in. The women were there to meet us, but had arrived two minutes too late. Phone calls were frantically being made to try and trace us. They had the police search the train down the line. Apparently a woman involved in anti-Ku Klux Klan work had been killed when she was thrown from that same train two weeks earlier. I sensed the fear very strongly of those working for justice in the South. It was a fear that was reinforced by the injustice of November '79 when the Ku Klux Klan and the Nazi party attacked a rally which was labelled as 'communist'. This resulted in the massacre of five demonstrators who were shot. Four television stations recorded the killings in awesome detail, but an all-white jury tried and acquitted the six men who carried out the murders. Some people chose to believe that the jury had learned things about that day that the rest of us will never know. Ku Klux Klan members are not discouraged from doing public relations jobs. They are allowed to recruit new members at their rallies. Children are constantly being influenced by the Klan, given phone numbers to ring whereupon Klan propaganda is relayed to them. The politics of the Klan includes extreme upholding of Christianity, heterosexuality of white-skinned people and the oppression of women. Anyone falling outside these categories is seen as perverse and unfit to live as part of so-called civilisation. I got very strong feelings over there, from myself and so many other people, that the Ku Klux Klan are another extension of American government policies.

The women organising the tour were so shaken by our disappearance that they arranged for martial arts experts to be at the meeting that night and for security to patrol the car parks.

With all this, my paranoia level was rising. Each time we spoke of these incidents we would get feedback of other people's experiences and our fear grew accordingly. One case was of a woman working for the War Resisters League. She was disturbed from sleep one night by a man in her bedroom. He ran off with her diary and address book. She was harassed for two months, followed each day, and whenever she arrived home there was a phone call, and a voice would remind her of all her activities during the day. She was cautioned and threatened about her work against state policies and other people in her address book got the same treatment.

Then, the last straw. Toni and I were on our way to a meeting. Judy, who was driving, just managed to keep the car safely on the road as another vehicle swung right across our path. I turned round just in time to see a man with a camera hanging out of the window of the car that nearly pushed us off the road.

We were all quite unwell by this stage. There were only four more days of the tour left. They had found another week of bookings. My nights were sleepless. I was afraid now, my paranoia and fear seeping through my consciousness and affecting my days. Toni gave way to her needs and flew back to London. We did one more meeting, cancelled the seventh week, and then retreated to the woods. Some beautiful women we had met earlier in the tour gave us the space we needed to rest. We had to take the phone off the hook. People were still calling to see if 'the Greenham women' would change their minds.

I still feel positive about the tour, even in the face of the pain that we travelled through. It was so much hard work and a thoroughly energy-draining process. The flow of communication between America and ourselves is growing stronger. Constantly I came across amazing and courageous actions that so many are involved in. I was surprised at what I found but clearly, it is in our Governments' interests to keep us in the dark, ignorant of each other's work against their life-destroying policies. So the control of press and other media keeps us apart. In that way, the tour has helped us cross a bridge.

A continual reinforcement of that communication is what's needed. The tour was also co-ordinated to be a build-up of interest and enthusiasm for Seneca Falls Women's Peace Camp where now thousands of women are involved in active resistance at the very place from which Cruise and Pershing missiles are shipped to Europe. So yes, it was worth me going all the way to America.

Women from Greenham have also travelled to many countries behind the 'Iron Curtain' to make connections with the human beings we are taught to hate and fear in order to justify the arms race. We hope to expose some of the myths that perpetuate hostility between East and West. *In July 1983 a group of women visited Hungary. Lynne Jones was one of them:*

The first time I saw it, it looked too small. A nine-foot-high concrete wall, barbed wire behind it and empty space. White mud stretching some hundred yards to another wall. This one with watchtowers and searchlights where impassive young soldiers stared down. A wall dividing a city, dividing a continent, dividing the world. And meaning . . . what?

These were my thoughts as I stared down from the S Bahn crossing from Friedrichstrasse to Berlin zoo. The children on the

131

Eastern side wrote essays describing it as the wall to keep out fascism. In the West, a whole group of leaders would be left quite speechless without it, using it as they do to symbolise our 'freedom', to justify the building of further fortifications back home. Not surprising really that no one wants to take it down. So while the electronic gates were going up and the barbed wire and searchlights were being extended around the base at Greenham to increase 'my security' at home, the least I could do, I thought, was cross over and see for myself what it was like on the other side.

We had heard about a peace camp being organised in Hungary, by a group of young people calling themselves the Peace Group for Dialogue. Before I go further I had better explain that peace movements do not work in the same way in Eastern Europe as they do here. Each country has a state-sponsored Peace Council whose role is to promote peace policy throughout the country. This policy is based on the view that the arms race, having been initiated by the United States, is being maintained by the West and that it is therefore up to the West to bring it to a halt. Weapons and conscription in the Warsaw Treaty countries are necessary for defensive purposes only and cannot be got rid of until the West stops striving for superiority.

This apparent one-sidedness, and the bureaucratic nature of the organisations, makes it easy for the West to portray them as a propaganda front for the Soviet Union's own arms stock. This ignores certain facts. These organisations have a membership of hundreds of thousands. Many people in Eastern Europe, re-membering their experience in the last war, genuinely perceive themselves as under attack from the West. Clear disarmament initiatives such as support for 'Nuclear Free Zones' and proposals for 'no first use' of nuclear weapons have been made by the Soviet Union, while the British Government has consistently opposed such proposals.

It is only recently that spontaneous and autonomous groupings have sprung up. They are more similar to our own western peace movements in their desire to look at militarism and the whole arms race. In East Germany, there is a movement of conscientious objectors, and a group of women protesting at women being drafted into the military. These groups are viewed with suspicion by the state and have been subject to some harassment. In Hungary, the Peace Group for Dialogue seemed, in the year of its existence, to have succeeded in demonstrating that it was possible for a

132

spontaneous and independent movement to grow side by side with the state-sponsored Peace Council.

They argued that the need for such a group came not from any desire to oppose or subvert the state, but from the need to challenge the idea that peace issues were solely the concern of bureaucratic organisations. They felt their autonomy and informal network of small groups generated a more genuine discussion among young people, especially on subjects like pacifism, and that it provided greater opportunities for grass roots contact with the West. The group, drawing its membership from school and university students, young workers and young married couples, had flourished and grown. Taking care not to do anything illegal and to work quite openly, it held a number of successful meetings with invited speakers from peace groups such as European Nuclear Disarmament and the Dutch International Peace Council. It had organised its own section of a youth march and held regular discussions with the Hungarian Peace Council on ways of working together. One such proposal made early in January was for a peace camp.

The idea was that young people from East and West would live together on a holiday camp site for a week to exchange ideas and discuss peace issues. Sara, Vicky, Jules, Katrin and I decided to go from Greenham to join them. We also wrote to the Peace Council saying we would like to visit them, too.

Since April 1983 however, relationships had soured. While the Dialogue had not itself changed, attitudes towards it had. Individuals began to be harassed. The Peace Council was less available for discussion and no longer appeared to be interested in supporting the proposed camp which was now proving difficult to get off the ground. One site, previously booked, turned out to be 'full', another 'closed'. A third site was found five days before the camp was due to begin and it was arranged that the visitors would be met at a railway station in Budapest. We arrived to find that 20 of the Hungarians wearing Dialogue badges had been picked up by the police. They were held for three hours. Those Hungarians who went directly to the site once again found it 'full'.

'Couldn't you take off your badges?' I asked in weary exasperation, after the fourth attempt to find a site failed.

'That is not our way. We have always been quite open about who we are because we are not doing anything illegal. It would be a big step to change our methods now,' said Ricky, one of the Hungarians. I felt justly rebuked. No one here was going to let themselves be pushed into cloak and dagger tactics.

On the third afternoon, while I was somewhere else, the other Greenham women were deported. It was only 12 fairly anxious hours later, when Sara rang me from Vienna, that I heard what had happened.

'Two plain-clothes policemen asked us to come with them to deal with some formality over registration,' she said. 'Of course, we went willingly, but they locked us in a small room for two-and-a-half hours. Then they told us to leave the country. We asked for an explanation, but they wouldn't give us one. After two more hours of protesting, they said if we didn't leave at once, we would be forcibly removed. The British Embassy told us they couldn't help at all.'

As the threat was being reinforced by the presence of police with truncheons, they agreed to leave, concerned if they resisted further, at what the repercussions for the Hungarians would be.

I did manage to see the Peace Council. Seven of us in a large formal room: five Hungarians from Dialogue, Joe from the Fellowship of Reconciliation and myself. We sat in high-backed chairs round a long white table. Bard Andras, head of the Hungarian Youth Peace Council, listened to our complaints.

He seemed as perplexed as ourselves by the week's events and didn't condone them but said from the point of view of the police, Dialogue is not yet a legal group.

'We are not illegal,' Mary argued angrily.

'Peace work can't be done by the Peace Council alone,' explained Julia, 'because it's lost the trust of the young. The decisions are made by high-ups and no one believes high-ups any more. Independence is important if we are to demonstrate that we are sincere.'

'Can't you see that allowing independent groups to exist can only strengthen your image in the West?' Joe argued.

'There are times,' replied Bard Andras, 'when, because our system is threatened, the social consensus is more important than the autonomy of little groups.'

The argument sounded strangely familiar. How often at Greenham had I heard that 'unity' in the face of Cruise missiles was more important than a women-only camp.

Forty Hungarians and Joe and I carried on the discussion in a single-room apartment. We were tired, perplexed and trying to decide what to do.

'The Soviet Union sees that the West is determined for the

Geneva talks to fail. It is looking for countermeasures such as the possible deployment of SS20s in Hungary. In which case, the last thing they want is Greenham women teaching us their tactics,' someone said.

'They shouldn't put us on the television, then,' I replied. Only an hour earlier I had seen Greenham women in front of police horses' hooves being beaten by truncheons – the July blockade. The newscaster had called them 'heroines' . . . strange irony. The evening wore on. The Hungarians sang, 'You can't kill the spirit . . . old and strong . . . she goes on and on.' Jules had taught them the words the night before she was deported. I wanted to cry. I needed to sleep. It was time to go home.

Coming home didn't solve my problems though. I wanted to tell people about what was happening, to gather support for Dialogue. Yet not everyone thought that was wise.

'Mention it and you can consider yourself directly responsible for bringing Cruise missiles one step closer,' a friend said. 'Can't you see this is just the kind of propaganda they want to justify yet more weapons? How do you know, anyway, that such groups aren't CIA agents themselves – put there to cause just this kind of trouble?'

'So you want me to start manipulating truth just like our friends on the Right?' I replied.

'Manipulation! Look Lynne, who dropped the bombs on Hiroshima and Nagasaki? Who has let out every stop in the arms race? Who went into Vietnam? Who murders human rights activists in El Salvador? And peace activists in Turkey? And where do you see that reported? All you ever hear is how evil the Russians are, how monstrous the system over there is, without any examination of our own. You want to add to that? The peace movement is supposed to be destroying the enemy image, not creating it!'

I understood what she was saying, but I simply wanted to be able to tell the whole truth. Too much goes unsaid.

'You're right,' I said. 'I can add to your list. What kind of freedom is there for people on the dole in Liverpool? How free are we to walk city streets at night? In Hungary there is full employment, I'm not scared of being mugged or attacked and I'm not assaulted by sexist adverts. People there are warm and friendly to total strangers in a way that you can't imagine, living here. But who is going to believe me when I say all that? When I say Eastern Europe is not the miserable, grey, oppressive place that it's painted to be, if I lie to cover up what is not so good?'

135

'Cruise is the only issue of importance right now. The Peace Council supports us in opposing it and they are not going to take kindly to your running around and interfering. You'll only offend them and drive us further apart.'

I sat then, stubborn, half of me agreeing. I had no desire to offend. On the contrary, while I didn't agree with everything Bard Andras said, I certainly wanted to go on talking to him. That was the whole point. Yet something in me balked. To serve my own ends in stopping Cruise, have I got to start holding up distorting mirrors? The kind that turn heroic trade unionists over there into dangerous subversives over here? That make freedom fighters into bomb-throwing terrorists and foreign intervention into fraternal aid? How does that help? My head spins. We justify our weapons by pointing to their repression. They say how can repression be avoided when you live in a state of siege, attacked on all sides? So 'freedom' is achieved by targeting missiles on those who struggle for that very thing, and peace by silencing those who call for it. How do you get out of the maze?

It would be easier if it was just the question of armaments. When the Soviet delegates met American peace activists recently, they said, 'We will not wait for you to solve your poverty and your racism before sitting down to arms discussions. You should not let our differences in human rights concern you, either.'

I wish that it could be like that. I wish the problems of the world could be dealt with separately, ticked off like items on a shopping list; armaments today, poverty, racism, women's rights tomorrow. But I don't think it's as simple as that. Cruise isn't the only problem, it's just a particularly pressing one.

There are others, I can name them: Auschwitz, Dachau, Hiroshima, Nagasaki, Mururoa, Christmas Island, Sharpeville, Diego Garcia, My Lai, Soweto, Chile, Nicaragua, Afghanistan, Cambodia, Lebanon, Seveso . . . The words toll like a bell in my head, a litany to destruction, conjuring up images of children screaming, houses burning, scarred faces, burning bodies, evictions, massacres, the air, the sea, the land itself poisoned and wasted. Cruise is just the latest symptom of a foul disease springing from a mentality that believes violence is the only way to solve conflict and that human beings, indeed all creatures, the earth itself, are expendable for short-term gain. It's a mentality that equates power with the ability to control others by force – with a fist, or money or a weapon. Such power can only be seized by the most aggressive,

136

ruthless and competitive person around. It's survival of the fittest, and don't shed a tear or you'll go under.

It is that mentality which is, for me, the real enemy. And it doesn't seem to be confined to either side of a wall that, in itself, springs from fear and distrust. Acid rain falls on both sides killing trees in Poland and Germany. Both sides operate a military draft. In our case, it's economic. Spend all your money on the military and what other job is there but the army? On both sides pacifists are accused and suffer for lack of 'patriotism'. Both sides sell armaments to other countries.

That is why I am at Greenham. Not just to stop Cruise, or Trident, or the Iowa Task Force, or the whole chain of horrors that come behind them, but to confront the idea that, in the face of all this, I am completely powerless. I am learning that I am not.

# 15
# Trials and Tribulations

It's late March and the wind still blows cold across 'injunction row'. Groups of women are huddled together around the fire, faces bleak and pale. The strain is showing in the hunched shoulders, in the way women stare deeply into the spitting flames. Conversation is short, tempers are short, we are too tired to care.

The women who have been away to Sicily, to Denmark and to Ireland, are slowly coming back. While they'd been away the relentless pressure had taken its toll. One woman had suffered a breakdown after her release from prison. Women tried to cope with it themselves, tried to find an alternative to the institutions that 'normalise'. After two intensive weeks of anxiety and search, an alternative crisis centre had been found. The woman was taken there and other women visited or stayed overnight to continue support. But after the fees had been paid, the crisis centre transferred her to a state institution without consulting us. We protested and she was eventually released on the understanding that two women would take responsibility for her. They took her to a cottage in Wales, to heal.

Media coverage of Greenham was now frequent and increasingly unsympathetic. Lots of prejudices were hurled our way showing the outside world's fear of lesbianism, politically active women and the search for women's powers.

The powers-that-be still indulge in whipping up prejudice to spur on those who will complete the task they have 'legitimately' initiated in the media.

*Jane's diary: 25 March* – We've been threatened with letter bombs now and we are having problems with marauding men in the middle of the night. Last night I was so frightened, I went through the worst imaginable thoughts of being murdered. The dog woke us, barking. We could hear footsteps all around the bender, then someone hit the bender with a stick, we were silent. A few minutes later we heard more footsteps and men's voices and we screamed and called for everyone. Anyway, by this time the police had come down as they'd seen something was going on and it was them we were screaming at which was a bit embarrassing.

CND were planning their first major direct action for the Easter weekend. On 31 March they planned a women's blockade at Greenham and a mixed blockade at Burghfield.

The following day, 1 April, was to be a symbolic action – a human chain of 14 miles, linking Greenham to Aldermaston (Atomic Weapons Research Establishment) and Burghfield. During the organisation for these events the differences between our campaigning strategies polarised. We are not convinced that marshalling large numbers in a conventionally organised manner is the best way to achieve our aims.

On top of all the other exhausting and upsetting things that had happened in the last weeks, this split meant more harsh words and hard feelings and it felt like everything was falling apart. We had been planning our own action for April Fool's Day. We felt that everyone, including the authorities, was becoming too confrontational, so that the establishment was becoming more able to legitimately use its power to repress.

So on 1 April, after a successful blockade on 31 March, 200 women, many dressed as furry animals, scampered into the base for a huge teddy bears' picnic. We undermined the security of the base yet again!

For ages we had been talking about how actions involving physical confrontation exhausted and, in some ways, damaged us. *Kim Smith is an ex-civil servant who had been working on a farm in Derbyshire. She'd moved to the camp in January '83:* We were looking for ways to close the base without womyn being dragged around and thrown into muddy ditches. Virtually in unison we said 'Citadel locks'. As anyone who rides a bicycle knows, Citadel locks are completely foolproof – if the key gets lost you may as well make your bike into a hatstand or some other useful ornament as they just can't be broken into.

The day before full moon on 27 April saw two of us dashing around all the big bike shops in London desperately trying to obtain locks. At 4.50 we panted into the only large bike shop that we hadn't tried and bought his last five Citadel locks.

Well we managed it, each of the gates was locked at roughly the same time – the Indigo Gate provided a few problems as Anna was chased away from the gate by the police, but as they were following her to Newbury, Jill and Arlene came along and put another lock on the gate. Most womyn then came straight back to the main gate to watch what would happen. One high-ranking policeman had managed to get himself shut on the wrong side of the gate and was obviously a bit put out by this – he prodded the lock and said that if we were going to do this sort of thing we may as well do it properly – we said we thought we had. The policeman inside then appeared with a pair of smallish boltcutters which cut cleanly through the rubber coating but made no impression on the lock. The policeman trotted off to get a hacksaw. The traffic was now building up outside the main gate – and being directed off to other gates which were also locked.

Return of officer with small hacksaw – he managed to remove the rest of the rubber from the area which he was trying to cut. By now there were all sorts of hysterical squeals coming out of the radios about large boltcutters. Enter two policemen struggling with a pair of boltcutters which were about five feet long. They placed the jaws of these around the lock and heaved on one handle each and then looked in utter amazement at the lock which wasn't even scratched. They carried on bouncing on the boltcutters for another few minutes and then gave up. Three large policemen then started to charge the gate to try and break the lock off. No good so they waved in reinforcements.

This time they got the gate open – but not in the way that was expected. The whole gate came away from the pillar on the right-hand side, swung gently in the breeze and then fell gracefully to the ground, connected to the rest of the fence by one gleaming and totally unscathed lock.

Once more the forces in the base had used their subtlety to deal with the situation!


At the camp, court cases were now becoming a regular event. Applications for legal aid were more often than not being refused as the verdicts of the local lay magistrates fell into a predictable pattern. But we continued to defend ourselves, challenging the transparent so-called system of justice. Our intention is not to alienate its ministers but to open their eyes.

These were two of the court appearances during April.

Jill Booth had been on a vigil outside Holloway prison. She was charged with 'offensive behaviour'. Her case was heard at Highbury Magistrates' Court in London and went something like this. The magistrate asked the policeman what happened. The policeman answered that on 25 February, 'I arrested the defendant for behaviour likely to cause a breach of the peace.'

'Would you explain what she was doing?' asked the magistrate politely.

'Yes, your honour,' replied the policeman. 'The defendant called me a wanker, your honour.'

At this the magistrate raised his eyes to the ceiling and took a deep breath.

'Yes?' he queried. 'Is that all?'

'Yes, your honour.'

'Would you kindly define the word "wanker",' said the magistrate patiently.

'I would rather not, your honour.' The policeman was beginning to squirm.

The magistrate, tersely, 'Well, I would like you to.'

There was an expectant hush as the policeman cleared his throat. 'It's someone who masturbates, your honour.' Muffled giggles from the spectators.

The magistrate then turned to Jill and said, 'Now Miss Booth, in your opinion would you say that calling someone a wanker is worse than calling them a b.f.?'

'Oh no, your honour,' said Jill, 'I personally have nothing against wanking. I was referring to his behaviour and attitude towards me as a human being and I was using the word in the sense that he was being mean, which he was.'

'Case dismissed.'

Another case set the tone for court hearings over the following months. *Nicky Edwards describes herself as a lapsed bureaucrat and a struggling writer. She was Becky Griffiths' 'McKenzie' (lay adviser) in court:*

They have put us in the smallest courtroom there is – Number 3. Upstairs in the large court there is one man being tried before an empty public gallery. Down here all but a handful of the women

141

who have come to support are excluded. We are almost resigned – it is no accident. They cannot see our lines of strength, but they know their presence, and blundering, try to cut them.

Becky and Paula are charged with causing a breach of the peace. They have taken down an American flag, which was flying over the base. They have no solicitor. We are getting so far outside their system, it seems pointless trying to woo their tolerance with legal politenesses. 'Can my McKenzie address the court?' 'No.' The clerk of the court revels in his power. He knows he will not be challenged by the laymen. When he oversteps himself too much (the magistrate had given her permission to go to the toilet, he gainsays it) he is gently reprimanded. But the policemen guarding the doors still take their orders from the clerk, not the magistrates.

I am Becky's McKenzie. The silent friend of the unrepresented accused. Allowed to sit at her shoulder suggesting questions, noting, rubbing her neck. But an amateur must not address the court (a conspiracy of gentlemanly lawyers to keep the dealing in women's freedom in their own hands has established that convention).

The prosecution starts his case by calling an American service cop. Paula is relaxed, the trial she knows will be a farce, she cannot take it seriously (although her questions will unsettle placid perjurers). Becky is shaking, with too many nerves left exposed by her last sentence in Holloway. The first witness passes unnoticed.

Nancy Lee Emory is called. There is hope in her. She is the American cop who seemed so sympathetic. Resignedly she lies on oath, not looking the women in the eye. She saw them throw the flag to the ground. Afterwards I ask her how she could do it. She looked tired. It was just one of those things, she said.

Airman Coverly is next in. A small timid cop, Nancy's sidekick. Becky asks her which country we are in. Airman Coverly fails to understand the question. She does not know what the British flag is called. For a full minute Becky leaves this ignorance painfully exposed, hanging in the air. But Airman Coverly knows whose base it is. 'The Americans are in charge,' she says. Oh yes, and admits that it is called RAF Greenham Common. An anachronism, obviously.

Who could have breached the peace? A problem this, for the prosecutor (or so we thought). Policemen and women couldn't be enraged to the point of violence, and who else was present? No one. So the fire station is called into existence, and a string of patriotic Yankee firemen testify to their outrage at the violation of their flag. Sergeant Hodges goes to the stand. He cannot read the oath. Sergeant Hodges cannot read at all. The muscles on the back of his neck bunch grotesquely as he affirms his belief in the flag of Hiroshima, Nagasaki, Vietnam. 'My country right or wrong.' He was not, it turns out, in a position to cause a breach of the peace, arriving after the women had been taken into custody by the US cops.

Sergeant Phillips comes to save the damaging admission. He was with Hodges and had to hold him back from attacking the women (he says). The fact that they were in police custody doesn't worry him (he looks contemptuously at the two policewomen, 'Pretty light protection'). Fireman Phillips was not there either when the potential breach of the peace was meant to be occurring.

Sergeant Hughes for the MOD police introduces the phrase on which the charge is to be hung. Becky, he claims, said to him, 'I will go back in there and do it again.' It is not true, but is enough. All the witnesses contradict each other on every other point, but they all have that phrase memorised off pat. Collusion, collusion, we sigh and sit lower in our seats. What's the point?

WPC Ford wants to use her notes. The women object and she stumbles, fluffing most of her lines except the one crucial damning phrase that she reproduces in the same form as all the others (weeks after the event she claimed she could not recall unaided).

PC Williams from Boscombe Down also wants to consult his notes. 'What time were they made?' he is asked. 'Just after the interview.' 'What time was that?' 'Just after it finished.' 'But what time?' He doesn't understand. This wasn't in the pre-trial team talk. He stands sweating and agonised, like a provincial actor struck with stage fright. The audience (magistrates, officials and police) grit their teeth and will him to make it. He cannot. Eventually the magistrate suggests a time to him. 'Shall we say half nine?' 'Yes, that's it,' Williams gasps, grasping the prompt in relief.

Becky goes into the witness box and reads an account of her action, its non-violence, its unplannedness; an anarchic, absurd spontaneity. The prosecution feels sure it must be an anti-American demonstration. He is an irrelevance in a goatee beard. Paula has nothing to say to the court – why should she bother?

Off go the three magistrates for a cup of tea and a decent interval before they come back to pass sentence. Do they count up to a thousand slowly? They mustn't be seen to be functioning on

143

auto-judge, but nothing touches them. The chairman of the magistrates is proud of his reputation as a reliable chap, who can handle these difficult women's cases. He is the prototype of a post WW3 public official – complacently administering the ashes by the rules. He is not there as a person any more. The first time he had to justify sending innocent peace women to prison, it may have caused him personal discomfort or even pain. It gets so much easier with repetition. Now the conscience has the ease of habit. He tells the women they are sending themselves to prison, it is not his responsibility.

They return to give sentence. Another day. Just routine. The clerk wants to silence Becky, but she knows her right to make a statement. She reads it – beautiful, strong. She is in tears. The words she uses to describe life and her love of it would be mawkish, if it weren't for the strength behind them. In tears, us in tears, them glazed. The chairman has warned that politics should not be allowed to intrude into this statement. The women are led away, hustled roughly. Two weeks in Holloway. What's two weeks to a busy public functionary? They know they are killing us. All done in an hour-and-a-half. Another day's work. ('Quieter than the New Year's trial'.)

Outside the police station, the Union Jack flies. We haul it down and throw it in the mud. No arrests are made, the flag is not ceremoniously burned because it has been defiled (unlike the stars and stripes which the women lowered). The policeman who eventually responds does not notice (or know) that he is hoisting our flag back upside down.

This story was set in England.


*Jenny Perringer's diary, 12 May, on the train to Newbury:*
Greenham is being evicted. I heard it on the radio while I was out buying a loaf of bread.

Transport always seems so unbearably slow at times like these! It will be all over by the time I get there.

That klunk, then panic on hearing the news, 'The Women's Peace Camp at Greenham Common is being evicted. Women are lying in the mud in front of bulldozers being dragged away by police.' And here is me so far away. Are they OK? Who's been arrested this time? I want to be there!

The last two evictions I've had to stay in London, watching it on

144

telly, stuck with work commitments here. Ugh, I feel so out of touch with Greenham. So difficult to juggle two lives, find a balance between my life in London and wanting to be living down there, doing absolutely everything I can. Where is the most politically effective place to be?

I'm worried about today. Bad time for an eviction. Even the *Guardian* is slagging off Greenham at the moment.

The eviction order granted at the High Court in March was finally being carried out. On a grey and drizzly Thursday morning, when a few early risers were brewing their first cup of tea, the bailiffs arrived. The alert call went out.

*Jane Dennett is a grandmother active in the Labour Party and retired from running her own small business. She had been living at the camp for several months and remembers being disturbed from a deep slumber early that morning:* I was sleeping in my car that night and I woke up hearing the eviction call and looked around. Unfortunately Beatrice's call of 'cooking pots' was louder than anyone else's, so I rushed to help Beatrice move the cooking pots. Young Pauline came over then shouting, 'Your car, they're taking your car.' I thought, 'My car? No.' Then I suddenly thought of my tent and the cooking pots and I became like that general in the war and I got on my horse and rode off in three different directions.

Jane got to her car, found the sheriff had the keys but luckily remembered a spare pair under the carpet. After a tussle, two of them clambered into the car, backed into a truckloader, and escaped.

*Jane:* We reached the main road where we saw a policeman on a motorbike and we thought he'd chase us, but I just drove madly to the house of a friend of mine, put the car into her back garden and put some blankets over it. Then my friend brought us back and we joined the blockade.

It was becoming clear to us how the Council intended to recoup the costs of the eviction. They would do this by impounding our cars, which, we later discovered, would not be returned unless we paid the sum of £3,000.

In all they took eight vehicles, and our response was not friendly.

Women climbed on to vehicles as they were being loaded on to the truck or towed away. They were violently pulled down. Two of the cars belonged to visitors but the police and bailiffs ignored our claims and rudely shoved women out of the way.

So we blockaded. Women sat, arms linked, some women with their children in their arms, lined across the roadway leading up to the main gate. We sat with our backs to the loaders, defying them to run us down.

That was an angry day – we were shocked as well as physically hurt by the aggressiveness of the bailiffs doing their 'Christian duty'. And later that night the television screens showed the public the violence we had been subjected to.

The following day support came flooding in. A busload of women arrived from Scotland early in the morning. They had been travelling the whole night and they stayed for two hours to let us know their support, then they got on their bus again and drove all the way back to Scotland.


It is now mid-May and new women are arriving to live at the camp. *Among them is Vickie McLafferty, whose expectations on arrival were shattered by the events which followed. One of these events is part of that thread of violence within each of us, that we are attempting to understand:*

From the very beginning things went wrong.

'Your ticket reads a half single, Glasgow to Reading. This train, my young lady, is a London train and you do not look under fourteen years of age,' spluttered the beer-bellied, bald ticket inspector.

'Oh,' said the would-be peace camper, who was promptly flung off the train at Euston Station.

I looked around the desolate station. I had that sense of 'I don't believe this'. There I was, less than 24 hours after leaving Uddingston Grammar School, in the middle of London on a Saturday night, no money, trying to get to Greenham Common Wimmin's Peace Camp which was somewhere near Reading which was somewhere in England. I lay down on a bench, convinced (by all the films that they show you in your fourth year at school warning you not to run away to London) that I would immediately become a heroin addict/child prostitute/vagrant.

'You cannot sleep here. It's against the rules. You've got to move!' Another spluttering British Rail employee.

'I'm not moving. I want to go to Newbury. I don't have any money. I'm tired. I'm not moving.'

Ten minutes later I was on a train to Newbury. Blockading the station bench had worked.

I arrived at camp having avoided being raped and pillaged by the Spanish lorry driver who gave me a lift, to see a group of about half a dozen women huddled round a camp fire. The next bit I don't like admitting: images of 30,000 women from 12 December flashing through my mind I marched towards the main gate; wondering who the shabby group round the fire were; and convinced that the 30,000 valiant peace campers I was about to join were on the other side of the fence. It would have been an interesting initiation ceremony had Christian Sarah called me a few seconds later and had the enthusiastic peace camper been arrested for visiting the base *before* she had visited the camp.

'Oi,' shouted a Glaswegian accent. I froze, convinced it was my mother and that I was about to be dragged by the earlobe back to school.

I walked over to the fire dragging my four suitcases behind me (I have three suitcases of toys, books, 'special' things which go everywhere with me and one suitcase with my sleeping bag and a clean pair of knickers). Sarah greeted me.

'Are you coming to stay for a while?'

I nodded, feeling like one of those poor, starving orphans you see in the weepy movies on a Saturday night, and wishing I was back in my bedroom with a plate of chips.

'Would you like some tea?' Sarah asked.

I muttered a yes. The next few minutes were wonderful and reassuring. Sarah and I discovered we had grown up in the same area and been to the same school, even thought there was a generation between us. Having failed three times to pinch a sandwich from the BR buffet I could contain it no longer.

'I'm 'ungry,' I burst out, to be treated to my first ever cooked-on-an-open-fire-eggy-toast, and guided, whimpering and with one eye open, to a bender. I can remember drifting into sleep thinking about meeting the other 29,000 women the next morning.

The next fortnight I spent adjusting to the camp and learning how to communicate with my own sex without being bitchy, envious, in competition with, etc. It was my first real encounter with feminism and having to face up to my own sexuality. It was beautiful.

It was two days after returning from Upper Heyford, an American airbase in Oxfordshire where F111 bombers are stationed, and where some of us had been taking part in blockades, that I noticed we had a violent woman in our midst. It was raining that morning: I remember having this terrible feeling that it wouldn't stop, that it would turn into a second flood. When I got up there was a fire burning despite the rain.

'Coffee,' I thought: there was no milk of course – every silver lining has a frayed edge. I went for a shit and came back to find the kettle boiling. Suddenly a woman jumped up, knocking quite a few chairs down, and kicked the kettle about 20 yards, narrowly missing Hiro's three-year-old son. It frightened me. Fear emanated from me like cheap perfume whenever I went near her after the incident.

A week later she broke my nose in two places. I said nothing to her, offended her in no way, it was just a case of my nose being in the wrong place at the wrong time.

I had retired to my bender, getting sympathy and hugs from Sarah and Tracey, when I heard her cursing and screaming and I ran out to see if she was hurting anyone. The camp was deserted. Everyone had retired to benders to evade her and recover from the violence. The scene was chaos. Two Canadian journalists had come to do an interview with women at the camp. They had stood looking at their feet for ten minutes before Cassie and Sally emerged from the newly erected information tent. Then all four had stood looking at each other's feet, whistling, commenting on the weather, embarrassed silence time.

Unfortunately this woman also emerged. She proceeded to kick over the few remaining chairs, thrust obscenities at the two journalists, laugh hysterically, tell the post box to 'stop winding me up'. Cassie, dressed in a pair of red pyjamas and a blue French beret with a huge turquoise feather, gesticulates, throws her arms up to heaven and screams in her usual dramatic fashion, 'It's all too much!'

Exit stage left of two scurrying, petrified Canadian journalists. How do you cope when strangers walk into a crisis in the middle of your living room?


*Barbara H.*: We didn't know. Nor was this the first crisis we'd had to deal with. Sometimes it feels like life is one long series of crises at Greenham. Living from day to day, not knowing whether your home will be standing tomorrow, makes for a very insecure life. The bottom line is that we have only ourselves in the end and we have a lot to learn about communicating with and supporting each other.

Many women have experiences and views different from Vickie's about this woman and how we didn't cope with her. The crisis had been building over a long period and was exacerbated by our inconsistent behaviour towards her. Several women had offered support, but they were not always available. We had no consensus on how to cope with her and most of us tried to pretend that it had nothing to do with us. She became a symbol of our fear of violence from others and a scapegoat for our own personal violence which we absorb through living in a violent, fearful world. That's what I mean by the thread of violence in each of us. This woman had come from a very brutal background – a vicious circle of violence at home, on the streets and from prison and mental institutions. These institutions had never helped her: they had merely thrown her back into the same vicious circle.

At a meeting once, where we were trying to work out how to deal with it, she was asked why she had come to Greenham. Her answer was direct.

'I came for a bit of peace.'

We couldn't give her what we ourselves didn't have.

# 16
# We Don't Want Your Wars!

24 May was International Women's Day for Disarmament. This was not a major event for us in terms of large numbers. Instead, this was the day when women across the globe demanded an end to oppression through war. Now women in all places were uniting in simultaneous actions in their hometowns to make our demand clear, 'We don't want your wars!'

Amongst thousands of other satisfying actions, 24 May gave birth to a women's peace camp at US/NATO Nuclear Submarine Tracking Station at Brawdy, Pembrokeshire, South Wales; another at Rosyth naval dockyard where nuclear submarines are refitted. Women in Scandinavian countries painted peace slogans on their blankets and hung them out of their windows. In Hartford, Connecticut, USA, two women wove a web around the headquarters of the largest US defence contractors. Police cut the web with knives and arrested the women. They made this statement: 'Women have traditionally made connections and men have consistently torn and destroyed them. We hope men will learn to make connections.'

In Harare, Zimbabwe, women held a peace cabaret. In Sydney, Australia, a motor cavalcade drove from the city centre to a nuclear reactor only 30 kilometres away, and set up a two-day peace camp. There were also actions against the Government's exploitation of Aborigines through uranium mining which blasts their homeland and uses their labour for work which often results in fatal contamination. A doctor in London, England, closed her practice and sat outside her surgery all day to draw public attention to the medical consequences of nuclear war. Women of Dorset, South England, set up placards outside Portland Underwater Weapons Establishment. In Auckland, New Zealand, a peace camp was set up at a naval base and 20,000 women marched through the city to draw the links between nuclear testing in the Pacific and deployment – the end of the nuclear chain.

Other actions included sit-ins at army recruitment offices, blockading a US spy base in Leeds, and women approaching their MPs on the nuclear issue. In some towns women took their children to visit their local emergency planning officers to ask what provision they had made for the safety of mothers and children in the event of a nuclear accident or exchange.

At Greenham, in respect for all those wonderful women, we had a day of silence and fasting. In the evening we received a message from the 24 May co-ordinating office in London: 'Over one million women took part in thousands of actions all over the world – actions involving from one or two women to several thousands.'

We were jubilant! All those women! The world was shown that women do not feel powerless. Women's growing concern and strength contrasts sharply with the repeated failure of male-dominated bodies to negotiate peace successfully.


There are lots of different ways to say no, and we have to try everything, from traditional reformist methods to non-violent direct action. Every door must be opened, every audience captured.

In May 1983, the local council elections were held. *Jane Dennett decided to pursue this path of reform and stood for a seat in the Newbury District Council, in the local ward of Greenham. She was backed by the Labour Party:* I obtained 147 votes. Not bad for a Greenham woman in a true-blue ward. The canvassing is obviously the 'big thing'. I found it took far more courage to knock on people's doors to ask them to vote for me, than speaking at meetings. Most people were reasonable, like 'You've got to be joking!' That's fine. I found it far more depressing to see how many women admitted to voting the same as their husbands, even when they were out of earshot.

Some were fatalistic (about Cruise). 'Well, we'll get it first,' they'd say. I replied by asking them what about their children and grandchildren? Often people would refer to God's will, which I thought a good start for an argument. Other statements were, 'This base is at the other side of town so it doesn't affect me' or, 'You don't know where to put your apostrophe so how can I vote for you?'

I often received very violent reactions. How do you cope? I survived by having lots of humour and showing it.

A few weeks later, on 9 June, the national elections were held.

*Rebecca Johnson was one of several women who stood as candidates to challenge particular Cabinet Ministers in their local electorates. She stood under the banner of 'Women for Life on Earth' and her experience tells us something about why our representatives often become distanced and unseeing about the problems in our everyday lives:* Any woman can stand for election, but the way the system is organised, it is a painful draining process and no woman could be blamed for not wanting to do it. I stood against the Secretary of State for War, Michael Heseltine. I have never felt so much in conflict with myself as during that time. I would wake up every morning with a sense of dread: to go up and down long driveways to knock on impersonal doors; to stand in markets and street corners talking through a distorting megaphone. No wonder the leaders 'we' (s)elect are so psychologically distorted. Again and again to go through that process, to have to suppress all natural consideration and sensitivity to impose oneself – it felt like invading. Once in a while on a doorstep the dawning consciousness . . . A letter received from someone who had been moved by a speech outside Thame Town Hall but hadn't dared to approach me . . . People excited and inspired after a meeting . . . but so few. The Henley constituency stretches from outside Reading to outside Oxford. The wealth and comfort seem untouched by poverty or unemployment. Three cars in a groomed driveway. The rejections were mostly polite and closed. The firm smile that is designed to put me in my place.

'I'm sorry but I don't agree with you dear.' This said before I had spoken.

They are so sure they know what I am about to say, what I think. Everything predetermined and complacent to minimise the necessity of questioning.

Words have been falsified.

'I think we need a strong defence.'

I used to think defence was something to protect us, putting our lives first, now it is a strategy for killing others with an acceptance of our own mass death as an (unfortunate) by-product.

'We have to be realistic.'

What is more realistic than recognising the stupidity and danger of nuclear war and attempting to avert it – not by turning to the failed prescriptions of the past and preparing for that unthinkable war in the vain hope that such a preparation will avert it? War has never been averted that way in history; only the anaesthetised could suppose that now it would be different.

Those polite dismissive phrases on the doorstep. And yet, every so often I saw a spark, a flicker. Someone fervently thanking me for standing – the first time she's been able to vote for someone she *agrees* with . . . she says she's 72. That's a long time to be disenfranchised.

On June 9 the Conservatives were returned to office. We felt pretty low . . . but not for long. We hadn't known the election would be in June and that we would need our spirits lifted. But, in tune with the cycle of the seasons, we had made plans to celebrate the full midsummer moon at the end of the month. A festival was just what we needed to revitalise us.

We wanted to create, with women's work, an enormous rainbow patchwork dragon that would stretch its tail around the base. It was inspired by women's work woven into the fence on 12 December 1982, but this time it would not be destroyed. We hoped it would become a living, travelling exhibition to symbolise women's hopes and our demand for peace. It would be another way of saying no.

The symbol of the dragon appears in mythology in many parts of the traditional world, such as China and the vandalised culture of the North American Indians. In Aboriginal Australia, the 'Rainbow Serpent' is a universally respected divinity who represents the eternal flow of life-forces or blood. S/he is seen in the undulations of the Australian landscape and certain places have been designated by the Aborigines as sacred ground.

The path of the Rainbow Serpent across Australia includes, not coincidentally, the uranium mines – land which has been stolen from the Aboriginal people.

The Aborigines tell a story, thousands of years old, which says that when the Rainbow Serpent is disturbed it will rise up and destroy the earth. Uranium, when it is exposed to light in open-cast mining, displays a kaleidoscope of colour – the colours of the rainbow.

We brought these ideas together in a Dragon Festival at Greenham on 25 June. A four-mile-long dragon was sewn together with patches sent to us from all over the world. The dragon is still travelling the globe.

# 17
# Insecurities

Just a few days later, on 4 July, we were back in action with a week-long blockade of the base which had been organised by London women. During this week, we cut the fence for the first time.

The blockade led us to rethink the form and impact of our actions. Blockading can be empowering and it can and does disrupt work at the base, but it can also be very distressing at times. We began to look for other fruitful ways of showing our opposition to what goes on in the base. We thought that one of the most useful things to do, would be to highlight the insecurity of the base. After all, an insecure base is virtually non-operational. It would also be a tremendous embarrassment to both the British and US governments when they have to admit that it's necessary to defend the base against those they are supposed to be defending! What they are protecting isn't for our benefit. It is their means of maintaining power over us and that's why, ultimately, they are prepared to shoot us to keep it.

On 23–24 July an Air Tattoo was held at USAF Greenham Common. It was an exhibition of NATO air arms put on to promote sales and public confidence in the military. Potential customers included Chile and Argentina.

Early on the morning of 25 July, while the 'exhibition pieces' were still under strict surveillance, seven women entered the base uninvited. It was a spontaneous action partly in response to our anger at this glorification of killing. It was to have more political significance than we were aware of at the time.

*Tracy Hammond, from the East End of London, was unemployed when she came to the camp. She describes what happened:* There was a group of us sitting in the bender, Suzannah, Juliet, Hilary and me, getting stoned, when I piped up with 'I want to paint a plane'. The

154

others thought it was a good idea, so we went off to the main fire and announced it. Another four women said they wouldn't mind doing it: Sarah, Ingrid, Georgina and Toma. So we got the boltcutters, and some paint.

We set off walking down the road and clambering through bushes and gorse until we came to the fence. Then we got lost. We had a discussion standing by the fence about which way to go, left or right, because everyone had lost their sense of direction. We decided to go left. Then we came upon these planes. It was dark but they had a spotlight there. And soldiers. So we sat in the bushes deciding what to do 'cos all we could see were these old World War Two planes and I got in a hump. I didn't want to paint them. Something about painting a monument, although it's still part of patriarchy, I didn't feel OK about. I wanted a big American plane.

Juliet went scuttering off down the fence to see if she could see any bigger planes. What happened next . . . well, there was this noise which sounded sort of electronic. Sarah was convinced that they had rigged up some sort of electrical device to freak everybody out. Suzannah was laughing so much Sarah was holding her head to the ground so she wouldn't be heard.

The electric device turned out to be a nightjar. It was even funnier when it flew out of the trees and everyone freaked out again.

We were just deciding what to do when Juliet came scuttling up the fence freaked out because she'd been lying in the bushes thinking she had been seen by soldiers. She decided not to come with us but agreed to bring the boltcutters back after we cut an 'ole in the fence.

As we got in, to the left of us, about 150 yards away there were these two big planes with US Air Force written on one of them. I said to Suzannah, 'them ones'. We made this almighty dash followed by the other five. I started spray painting, Suzannah threw half a tin of red paint over it and most of the other half over me. This American was reading his paper and he walked around the nose of the plane and shouted 'Stop!' but we all just continued painting women's symbols, writing LIFE, and Sarah was doing crosses.

A soldier with a dog came and moved us all away from the plane. So we just started dancing and singing and painting on the runway where we were. The soldiers were shocked, but since they're not allowed to talk to us they didn't say anything after they told us to

155

stop. Then the MOD police arrived and more soldiers.

I was standing next to Sarah quite happily painting the runway when this BIG policeman came up to me and took the paintbrush and asked me my name. I looked up at him and smiled and he said, 'Oh, Tracy Hammond'. He then went to Sarah and said, 'And Sarah Hipperson, criminal damage'. One of the MOD police said, 'Kick 'em all out' so one of us had to point out to them that we had actually painted the planes. He then said, 'Criminal damage, the lot of you!' (PS We didn't know we had done the Blackbird spy plane, the world's finest (and most expensive) until ITV dragged us out of bed after our release the next morning. The whole camp was in uproar. We had a party. Who told them? We didn't. It was announced in the paper that £¼ million's worth of damage had been done. In the end we heard from an MOD source that it took them about £2½ million to get the plane back in working order. The charges were later dropped. I was furious.)

It was a cover up. Neither the British nor the Americans wanted to admit responsibility for security so no charges were pressed. The fact that there was no trial meant the embarrassing insecurity of the base, and the admission that the Americans have ultimate control of it, was never publicly aired or questioned. A court hearing would also have exposed the ease with which such highly sophisticated weaponry can be demobilised. In addition, the amount of damage would have had to be openly discussed in court. This would have revealed the technique of using special titanium coating on the aircraft which provides a heat shield and resistance to radar detection.

This cover up has persisted. There are continual breaches of security that are not reported to the civil police so the public never receive the information about the base's vulnerability.

*Barbara's diary: 26 July* – Women went into the base in the early hours with spraycans but they got nervous and ditched the paint . . . then wandered around for hours, went into a mess kitchen and made coffee – all without being detected – until they got bored and came out again.

Security . . . what a laugh!

*24 August* – Grannies for peace have been staying here for a few nights and early on the last morning popped into the base to put up a flag. They were caught and tried the same morning. Becky, Tracy

156

and Leslie have been in just about every night, mostly without getting caught. Tracy and Becky went in one night and switched one of the generators off and lights around the silos went off. They also saw signs near the silos, which were still covered up, saying 'You are now entering an area covered by the Official Secrets Act' and that there are armed guards patrolling the area.

Our own securities were being tested too as people's fear of us and what we stand for was being acted out.

A few months earlier an occasional car would pass with jeering men shouting abusive slogans like 'fucking lesbian cunts' or 'we want Cruise'. Firecrackers were thrown from passing vehicles amongst the women sitting around the fireplace near the highway. Once a bottle of diluted acid was lobbed over. Sometimes, after pub closing time, a few men would arrive and park on the opposite side of the road and jeer from a safe distance or, at a later hour, having parked more discreetly down the road, would creep into the camp and throw paint over our benders.

Gradually, the abuse hurled from passing cars became a daily occurrence. The attacks were not just to intimidate, and they had nothing to do with Cruise missiles.

In late July, the organiser of 'Greenham Women Out' stated on television that the responsibility for getting rid of the camp lay with the Government. But if they did nothing about it then members of the public would be forced to take their own action – action for which they could not possibly be responsible, as that responsibility lay with the Government.

Several times warnings were issued to women that vigilantes were coming. Posters appeared in pubs in Newbury (pubs from which camp women and supporters have been excluded). One such poster invited people to 'come and join the vigilante group'.

During July and August we had containers of maggots, blood and faeces thrown over the benders. Tents were trampled over and slashed with knives. Quick-drying cement was poured into the water supply and the standpipe was stolen. Women were attacked – two women were sprayed with blue dye.

One night two fires were started by vigilantes. One was near a new encampment at the Orange Gate and came within 25 yards of a fuel dump. The other was in the gorse bushes beside the main gate and came within feet of the plastic-covered benders.

We are determined not to be provoked, but it isn't easy. The danger we face is now on both sides of the fence.

Did you know that 25 per cent of all violent crime is wife assault?[1]

New encampments were now starting up all round the base. In response to this, council harassment was being stepped up. Evictions from every camp except the main gate were becoming a weekly event and we, in turn, became more mobile and more adept at repitching camp.

# 18
# De-fencing

What we have learnt, by going inside the base, is about crossing artificial barriers. By overcoming our fear of the authority the fence represents, the fence itself becomes useless as a form of security.

De-fencing is the removal of barriers that divide us and thereby accommodate conflict.

On 29 October we invited women to join us in removing one of these barriers.

*Theresa:* Taking down the fence was, for me, a most powerful celebration, and expression of 'No'. 'No' to the machine and the barriers it creates, the fence being a visible, physical barrier but 'No' also to those invisible ones that keep us so alienated, East from West, black from white, heterosexual from homosexual, barriers of class, religion, barriers of privilege and deprivation. The strongest realisation I had before breaking away their barrier of chainlink fencing was that we had entered a time of massive irreversible change and that this action would somehow be the seal of this change. Sitting on top of Babs' shoulders cutting away the taut and tensioned wires, knowing after a few clumsy but willing attempts, exactly where to cut to allow the tension to be released, I felt completely calm. I knew when I was up there that we were opening up something very big, exposing a nerve so sensitive and afraid without its protective layer, allowing the fresh and healing air to pass through, being able to see clearly the causes of all this pain and illness and for the first time staring it right in the face, able to confront and deal with this monster machine.

On Saturday, 29 October women came to Greenham with a similar vision. The build-up through the day as women arrived was magical, so calm, warm, encompassing more and more arriving women. We had no rigid practical plans as to how the day would work. The fence around the base had been divided into the twelve signs of the Zodiac and women could use this in whatever way felt best for them. The thirteenth sign – Arachne – 'the spider', after two thousand years of lying dormant, had a comeback.

There were a series of meetings at the camp starting five days before the 29th. The idea for spider originally was that it would be a central point where there would be various practical and legal workshops, information, fearsharing. Spider was also to be a registration point to assess the numbers of women and from that information we could work out how many there were to cover the distances between the signs of the Zodiac.

We had agreed that the time to start would be around 4 p.m., but some women felt that even this was too rigid and would take the initiative away from women. Many hours we talked, eventually reaching a consensus that around 4 o'clock was how we'd like it to be. The vision of women working together on the fence was very powerful and starting at different times would alert police and military. Also, in the preceding weeks we had been travelling the country talking with women's groups and many had already been given the time of 4.30.

The role of spider as a registration point was disputed strongly. Here was a space, it was believed, where women could assume positions of power, where women wanting to control and manipulate would gather. Also, if there were to be any police infiltrators they would know exactly where to come. The meeting was incredibly hard – many women would feel reassured if Spider existed, while others felt devastated by the need and possible role of it. Around and around we went, each woman expressing her feelings.

For me the build-up of feelings for and against was very painful but what I did get out of it was a belief that this action would work. I was ready, having travelled through my fears, prepared and believing that I/we would take down the fence. And with this belief I didn't need to know how many women were here. When Babs was on my shoulders snipping away at the wire it felt good to know that women who had come were as individual women saying 'No' in their own way and not as part of a calculated operation. We still had workshops, and instead of a central Spider we had mobile spiders travelling around the signs of the Zodiac gathering and sharing information and each woman we shared it with also became a spider. Other women covered each of the signs, all of us connecting with each other, working and coming together on our vision.

One woman was stopped and arrested at 2.30 in the afternoon. The police had spotted her boltcutters. But the police, where were they? They knew something was going on, the military too, for they had set up camp around the inside of the fence. I'd expected at least a raid on the camp in the days leading up to the action. It was possible, it seemed, that they would arrest women at the camp for conspiracy, but no sign of them. Car and coachloads of women could have been stopped, searched, and arrested for intent. I heard of one coach travelling from Glasgow being stopped and searched in Carlisle. The police found a pair of ladders and apparently pleased with their discovery they waved the women on. We had been planning this action for months. Women going out talking, women going out shopping for 'black cardigans' – boltcutters. When women went shopping people became curious. 'Are you from Greenham?' they began to ask. One shop where we had ordered some boltcutters phoned up the factory to ask what the delay was and he was told the factory had stopped producing them.

The time came to move towards our chosen area at the fence. I was with a group of seven women, four of us cutting and a legal observer. Women were appearing from out of the woods and bracken, moving to their chosen places. Silently and calmly we began to tie balloons and streamers to the wire. The soldiers looked completely bewildered, looking to us, to each other, wondering what was happening. Their usual chorus of mindless prattling and insults didn't exist, their silence was ours. As the boltcutters appeared and we began cutting, they stood rooted in amazement. One soldier did move towards the fence but a small voice called him away. 'We can't do a thing,' I heard the voice say. The feeling was amazing. Up and down on each other's shoulders, so efficient, so sure, flying along the fence, releasing the tension until eventually I was plucked from Babs' shoulders. Two policemen had arrived and for the next 12 hours police stations, cells, processing, interrogation, the police station filling up with more and more women. And for 12 hours sending out energy to those women I knew would still be working on the fence. At 2.30 in the morning women were still coming into the police station.

Sharing our different experiences later showed us that the reactions of soldiers and police had been different all around the base. The army, British and American, had come outside the fence to arrest and injure women, dragging them through barbed wire, poking metal and wooden stakes through the fence at hands, breasts, faces; twisting arms and wrists enough to break them.

In one area at the fence an American in plain clothes, who was apparently commanding the operation, dealt out a karate chop to a woman's knuckles. When he left the British soldiers began helping the women to take down the fence. Others just stared in silence and rooted amazement. The tension between British and American soldiers is becoming more serious and the uncertainty is showing.

Two days after the 29th, British soldiers brought us a tree stump: on it was carved a peace sign and a message of hope. They were then reprimanded. The orders are to have no communication with women. This is backed up by fines and cancellation of leave. A policeman spoke words of encouragement for our actions to me.

And yes, now they've said they'll shoot us and the vultures are circling around, believing that the stage is set. But I ain't dying for you. That's what I came here to say. And when they come running with accusations of failure, I say we have all been failed and the decision to stop was always theirs, could only be theirs. And if they had stopped would it have been the end? No, it's only the beginning, this time of acknowledging nightmares, confronting fears, has prepared me for this, and my dreams have no end. The candle and the flame inside burning, still willing, still hoping, can only continue to enflame and rekindle another's passion and together we are powerful, more powerful than the machinery.

We have to come to terms with the stronghold of the military machine and the fact that it is never going to be easy to hold it back. We also have to assert that we will not be defeated, by reminding ourselves of our successes in the past and recognising our potential for the future. Nevertheless, the arrival of some of the Cruise missiles on 14 November 1983 was an unhappy day at Greenham.

*Soss Hancock first came to Greenham in early 1982. She had just started a new job setting up a girls' refuge in Edinburgh. She is still doing this work part-time, to fit in with her continued commitment to Greenham. She was at the camp when some of the missile bodies were flown in:* Yes, the missiles are here but they have been here all along. The mentality that has made them has been here all along. All around us and in us. And it's that we have to root out and go on struggling with. The people in the Pacific have already suffered the Holocaust, they have gone on resisting, resisting. And the

162

Aboriginal people and the Bush people of the Kalahari desert, surviving in the very heart of the desert where no other people can live, the rest of their tribe decimated. But their spirit has survived. The earliest people, those who really knew how to live co-operatively and with deep respect for the earth. We are learning. Nicaragua. Three million people have taken on the whole American war machine and they will not be defeated.

Ordinary womyn, animated and purposeful with the struggle of their own survival. We are part of the resistance. We are one current in the river. Landbased Cruise are arriving. Today is the beginning of a dangerous winter but we will see Spring. There are already sea-based missiles in the Holy Loch. We will have a womyn's action in the New Year. We will look 1984 in the eye. And we will not go under. We will strengthen our resolve and deepen our commitment to the total change that will be necessary to create the world we must have if we are to survive and live creatively.


On the same day, 14 November, in another member country of NATO, 23 people were sentenced, to up to eight years hard labour for working for peace.

The country was Turkey and these people are members of the Turkish Peace Association. Their average age is 50. Some of them are seriously ill and one has cancer. These people are also leading members of virtually every profession including an ambassador, a lawyer, a painter and an educationalist. They are to be examples to discourage dissension among others in their professions. 'They were put on trial just for the views they held, views no different to those expressed by CND in Britain.'[1] The sentences were passed by a military tribunal days after the November elections which were claimed to have restored Turkey to a democracy.

What is happening in Turkey does not exclude us, it warns us and exposes the system of terrorisation that protects the status quo. We must never be frightened into silence by the repression we witness, we must raise our voices for its victims! And we must consciously own, rather than disown, their struggle, for it is by breaking the silence that we break the divisions that keep us apart and powerless.

Lisa wrote to the TPA in London after reading a report in the *Guardian* that merely mentioned the sentencing of the peaceworkers . . . another body count. She wanted to learn more. This is the letter she received in reply.

Dear Lisa,

. . . I received your letter after almost two weeks of manic activity to subdue my pain and anger, to channel it to what matters most: to get my father and others out of that concrete coffin where they are locked in.

. . . My dad is President of the TPA. I became friends with him in a special way from the age of six when we ended up as a one-parent family. . . We travelled the world together, had our differences, had the kind of times which few kids can imagine. It was fun and exciting.

. . . The pain and anger I felt, therefore, wasn't just that of a peace-worker and a son but something very special. And that is when your wonderful letter arrived. . . I wept when I read your letter to say 'yes, there is hope for life, yes all this motion/ commotion is worth it!' Your letter made me feel strong, the same way as Greenham Common women have made women feel strong and men think. I thank you with all my consciousness for the moment of strength which your caring letter has given me. I have shared this with others – in particular Turkish women who have had to flee their homes and loved ones to seek asylum in this country. . .

Enclosed is information which reads like something out of a Hammer Horror film, typewritten on white pages. Each sentence is 'worked out': mustn't be too long, must be factual, don't show too much feeling otherwise someone might say it's 'propaganda'. Your letter says it all.

Bless you

Mar Dikerdem
(Dr Mehmet Ali Dikerdem)

When people are punished for peace-working in their own communities, how can their punishers be trusted or expected to make positive steps towards a peaceful world? Peace is their enemy – it means the end of our rulers' exploiters' power. They will not do it. It is up to us.

# Epilogue

*Katrina: December 1981* – The tipi is dark, women are sitting in a circle around the fire. Every now and then the smoke becomes too intense. We are holding hands, breathing deeply, aware of who we are, why we are here. We are powerful, we are here to stop Cruise missiles.

It is a few weeks later . . . the objects I have made and love are on the walls of the tipi. A woman's face full of love that I have painted looks out from the cloth wall. Other women's hangings line the tipi. I speak up and there are both men and women in the tipi. My voice is firm but nervous. I sense there will be criticism. I ask for the tipi to be a place for women only. For Sarah (who lives in the tipi) that is all right. There are rumblings from several of the men. We are just beginning.

It's February 1982. I come down to the peace camp. The rumblings of the men are louder. We are in a circle, the men's voices are full of anger, accusation – jealous and envious. Their voices intone again and again against the camp becoming women only. But the women's voices, those women who want the camp to be women only, are stronger and angrier. Sarah speaks about 'why women only' in a voice where words are tumbling out. The words are coming from deep down. Silenced words bursting out, gathering strength the more women say that we need to work with women. There is a meeting of all camp members in a caravan. I wait outside with a group of women and we concentrate on the camp becoming for women. There is too much at stake and it all hangs on too thin a thread. I feel such anger at the prospect of being silenced again, that the camp might not be a place where women can gather confidence. That the women's strength that is growing here might be crushed when it is the only thing that can stop Cruise missiles and the male domination of our Earth. I understand, I know what has turned our Earth into a technological nightmare. I know why I cannot walk at night without feeling threatened by attack. I know why there is militarism and imperialism and racism and sexism. I know why all the negative 'isms' exist. It's because of patriarchy – male rule.

A woman comes out. It has been 'agreed' by the men that the camp 'may' be 'women only' for 'two weeks leading up to the eviction'. There is a deep sigh of relief from women waiting outside. The Women's Peace Camp never looked back. Women fought for the right to work with other women, and argued often with other women who didn't understand.

A writer on women and madness has said that women are 'emotionally malnutritioned'. I have kept on thinking about this phrase ever since I first read it. I know it to be true. Stating that we are oppressed does not heal the wound. There are millions of everyday ordinary ways in which we are drained of our energy, used and manipulated by men. And the most enraging hurt is the way we have been denied, and our needs have been ignored so much that we cannot say what we want any more.

That's oppression, not to know as a woman that you are oppressed! The sense of the hurt comes from the gut and comes out in such bitterness and anger.

> Bitter-eyed women, slit-eyed women, laughing, laughing, but it's not funny. Raging to tear up the roots of friendships with ferocious teeth.

Never mind about the 'big politics', the personal draining of women's life energy is going on all the time, slowly and painfully in the home, on the street in 'paid' work. In the western countries there is the emotional malnutrition of women; in the rest of the economically oppressed world there is the acute emotional and physical malnutrition of women and children and men. So, we have to take our power, assert our rights, demand that our needs are fulfilled; and if we don't we will be trampled all over by men's dominant need to take everything we have – our power, our life's energy, our life's blood. We are raging women.

In the struggle for women to have the room to express our full power and become a truly women's peace camp, men did not give up their power. Women took our power. So much has divided us as women. We've been separated by race and class, lesbians have been separated from heterosexual women, Christian women from witches, the 'mothers' from prostitutes. The divide is chasms deep

166

and the chasms cannot be papered over. Real healing needs to be done, respecting the need for women of different races and classes to organise together autonomously. It starts with me.

*March 1982* – A women's blockade has blocked off all the gates to the base but the military open up a gap in the fence. Women rush to block the gap and immediately 33 women are arrested. The gap becomes known as the black hole. But there are several women left and they stay there, chanting from deep within them, looking each policeman straight in the eye. Something is happening. They are powerful, not to be moved easily. Women join in, the power grows. At 5 o'clock, after having moved several times, there is a crescendo of powerful voices ringing out . . .

<blockquote>
Women, Women, Women<br>
we've only just started!
</blockquote>

The March action carries me on to visit in the summer. I come down from our small, tightly knit group of women outside Waddington Nuclear Base in Lincolnshire. Greenham gave me the strength to branch out, to set up somewhere else. The camp is blossoming, a women's culture is growing. It's brightly coloured, confident and new. We spin webs across the gates, sing out with new songs, learn to juggle and blockade the main gates for two weeks. There is a hotch potch of activity. Lesbians are confident here and this is a sign of our growing stronger. The atmosphere is excitable, like shedding a dowdy skin and emerging vividly painted. The sense of our power is intoxicating. It's a bonding, but it's not idyllic. A power imbalance always constant, instilled deep within ourselves, drifts around the camp. It stills the words 'us' and 'we' in my mouth and puts the word 'you' in their place. 'How long have you lived here?' I'm asked the fatal question. 'I'm just visiting,' I say. I still say, 'What will you do?' to other camp women when talking about the camp. Unconfident, not desiring to be forward, how often we understate our role until we wipe ourselves out of existence.

As more women come and go, this mental self-depreciation becomes easier to cope with. We are all women working for change. It's not a question of what *you* will do, as though a few lonely leaders will face a reactionary onslaught. It's what 'we' will do, what we have done and are doing. And if I distance myself by seeing peace camp women only as women who have lived there a certain time, what a putting down of other women and myself. And what a lonely pedestal to be knocked off, those select women on it. The power has to be equal, to be shared, circling around the large network of women, all equal, but with different strengths and weaknesses. Each one of us has a different flavour of power and is working in separate areas that make up the whole. Without that there is no whole.

We are facing male power. The cells are tomb-like, condensation runs down the walls. We call out to the policewomen: 'Could you leave the window flap open?' There are six or so women in a small cell. We are choking on each other's breathing out. The policewoman can't leave the window flap open, can't let us use a proper private toilet, and it's more than her job is worth if she leaves the door open. It's 1 and 2 January. February, March, April, May, or June. It's all the times women have been arrested and locked up. Trapped. We are on a motorway in a police van with lights flashing on our way to Holloway at 80 miles an hour. We are threatening, dangerous women bawling out our songs at 80 miles an hour down the motorway. We are in Hollow-way, give up hope, and we are lucky! Only two weeks. This is at the heart of their power. A place where we have no dignity, where we are strip-searched, locked in and insulted. They are very frightened of us.

The lorries grind on, building the silos. Mechanical power that roars past women lying in its way. Brute power that drags women away from a blockade. Bit by bit against our will the silos are being built. My will is locked on those silos. I have an iron will, a furious grip. It shall not happen. We grasp what damage is being done with the whole of our beings. 12 December. Powerful, determined, I stand with thousands of other women when the Earth is barren and the wind is blasting. We turn away from the silos with a grim look when the sun is setting in the Spring. Summer, Autumn and Winter. The cycle of seasons passes and we are still there, nourished and nurtured by each day to oppose the evil behind that fence. We are stronger than the military. We will survive.

# Notes

*Chapter 14: Talking Through Our Trips to Other Places (pp. 114 – 137)*

1. See resource list at back of book for further reading.
2. On 13 December 1983 one British newspaper, the *Morning Star*, revealed that upwards of 10,000 plastic bullets were in the hands of the Metropolitan Police. Their use in Britain was authorised after the 1981 riots, such as in Toxteth and Brixton. In some areas local police authorities have ordered their forces to get rid of these weapons but the Home Office retains the power to insist on their use. For further information, contact Campaign Against Plastic Bullets, c/o BSSRS, 9 Poland Street, London W1.

*Chapter 17: Insecurities (pp. 154 – 158)*

1. Counter Information Services, No. 28, *Women in the Eighties*, p. 4.

*Chapter 18: De-fencing (pp. 159 – 164)*

1. Euro MPS Roland Boyes and Ann Clwyd who visited TPA executive when they were out on bail in September 1983.

# Resources

*Books*

Cambridge Women's Peace Collective, *My Country is the Whole World*, London, Pandora, 1984.

Alice Cook and Gwyn Kirk, *Greenham Women Everywhere*, London, Pluto, 1983.

Mary Daly, *Gyn/Ecology: the Metaethics of Radical Feminism*, London, The Women's Press, 1979.

Andrea Dworkin, *Woman-Hating*, New York, E. P. Dutton, 1974.

Charlotte Perkins Gilman, *The Charlotte Perkins Gilman Reader: The Yellow Wallpaper and Other Stories*, London, The Women's Press, 1981.

Susan Griffin, *Woman and Nature: the Roaring Inside Her*, London, The Women's Press, 1984.

Lynne Jones, *Keeping the Peace: Women's Peace Handbook*, London, The Women's Press, 1983.

Pam McAllister (ed), *Reweaving the Web of Life: Feminism and Non-violence*, Philadelphia, New Society, 1982.

Marge Piercy, *Woman on the Edge of Time*, London, The Women's Press, 1979.

Elizabeth Sigmund, *Rage Against the Dying: Campaign against Chemical and Biological Warfare*, London, Pluto, 1980.

*Ireland*

Margaretta D'Arcy, *Tell Them Everything*, London, Pluto, 1981.

Eamonn McCann, *War and an Irish Town*, London, Pluto, 1980.

Belinda Probert, *Beyond Orange and Green*, London, Zed Press, 1978.

*Falklands*

Ecoropa Information Sheet II, Crickhowell, Powys NP8 1TA.

David Tinker, *A Message from the Falklands*, Harmondsworth, Penguin, 1983.

*Pamphlets*

'Black Women and the Peace Movement', Wilmette Brown, available from

King's Cross Women's Centre, 71 Tonbridge St, London WC1.

'Breaching the Peace', London, Onlywomen Press, 1983: a criticism of the women's peace movement, some of which has been addressed in this book.

'The British Media and Ireland: Truth, the First Casualty', available from Campaign for Free Speech on Ireland, 1 North End Rd, London W14, 70p.

'The Greenham Factor', Greenham Print Prop, 1983.

'Piecing it Together: Feminism and Non-violence', Feminism and Non-violence Study Group, 1983, available by post from Feminism and Non-violence Study Group, 2 College Close, Buckleigh, Westwood Ho, Devon EX39 1BL.

## Magazines/Papers

*Lysistrata*, 7 Florence Rd, Brighton, Sussex.

*New Statesman*, 10 Great Turnstile, London WC1V.

*Outwrite*, Oxford House, Derbyshire Street, London E2.

*Peace News*, 8 Elm Avenue, Nottingham 3.

*Radiator*, 43 St Marks Rd, Salisbury, Wiltshire.

*Sanity*, 11 Goodwin St, London N4.

*Spare Rib*, 27 Clerkenwell Close, London EC1.

## Films and Videos

'Carry Greenham Home', made by Amanda Richardson and Beeban Kidron who lived at Greenham for several months; an honest representation that doesn't seek to propagandise.

'Commonsense: Actions 1982', Gwynn Kirk. Some Greenham actions.

## Addresses

Armagh–London Group, 374 Grays Inn Rd, London WC1.

Campaign Against the Arms Trade, 5 Caledonian Rd, London N1.

Campaign for Nuclear Disarmament, 11 Goodwin St, London N4.

Greenham London Office; tel: 01–833 2831.

Greenham Women Against Cruise, 5 Leonard St, London E16; tel: 01–251 8046.

National Council for Civil Liberties, 21 Tabard St, London SE1.

SWAPO Women's Solidarity Campaign, 53 Leverton St, London NW5; tel: 01–267 1941/2.

Turkish Peace Association, 13 Bolton Walk, Andover Estate, London N7; tel: 01–263 4476.

Women's Peace Alliance, Box 240, Peace News, 8 Elm Avenue, Nottingham.

Women's Peace Camp, USAF Greenham Common, Newbury, Berkshire.